"Move over Franklin-Covey!"

—John Chamberlain
Environmental Consultant, SRI International

"If you feel like you are drowning in paper and projects, you need The Naked Desk. *Filled with wise, practical tips for managing tasks and time, Sue Brenner's book will help you get done what matters at work so you'll have time for the rest of your life. Get it now and start turning your piles into smiles!"*

—C.J. Hayden, Author
Get Clients Now! and *Get Hired Now!*

"When you read The Naked Desk, *you'll be amazed at the wealth of smart, simple steps she offers. And, you'll want to pass on these tips to everyone you know."*

—Jerry Pujals, CEO, Author
Secrets to Real Estate Success and *Kick it Up a Notch Marketing*

"Thank all the heavens that be for Sue Brenner's book, The Naked Desk. *Buy this book NOW! and read it each and every day. You will be glad you did!"*

—Joanne Victoria, Author
Vision With a Capital V

"The Naked Desk is a thought provoking, power-packed book with no fluff. Apply just five steps from this book and you'll experience more fulfillment at work with fewer things in the way of success."

—Judy Cullins, Author
Write Your eBook or Other Short Book—Fast!

the [n]aked desk

SUE BRENNER

the [n]aked desk

SUE BRENNER

IGNITE
PRESS

Note

The stories that inspired this book feature real people. However, the names and identifying details have been changed to maintain confidentiality.

ISBN 978-0-9789730-0-1

ISBN 0-9789730-0-3

Cover and Interior Design: *AuthorSupport.com*

Cover Photography: *PhotoAlto*

For my husband, Doron—thank you for being a sounding board and inspiring me every step of the way.

For my daughter, Kayla—your joy brightens every day.

Table of Contents

Introduction

Do stacks of paper pile up on your desk? Do your work days get longer and longer? Do you run around trying to accomplish things, but never seem to get ahead? Does procrastination hover over your desk like a back-to-life dinosaur waiting to eat you?

At wit's end, you think, "There must be a better way." An easier way to get organized, gain time (and life!), and stop procrastinating. There is. You *can* enjoy work more and feel that your life matters. You *can* leave work at 5:00 p.m. (not 8:00 p.m.). You *can* spend quality time with your family, get ahead in your job, and do your best at work—without collapsing in a heap at the end of the day.

The Naked Desk strips through the stuff that gets in the way—clutter, disorder, unproductive busy-ness, procrastination, "back-burner" projects that tug at you. It offers what you need to stop struggling and start flourishing.

With humor and enthusiasm, each chapter gives you direct, no-nonsense ways to overcome obstacles and get organized. For example, glimpse at Chapter 4: *The Top 5 Procrastination Traps—and What to Do About Them*. There you'll find fun, easy ways to unbind you from the specific traps that lead to procrastination.

Enjoy the original action steps that will help you pave the way to success, without leaving your heart behind or burning out. You'll discover how to access the greatness you already have—and apply it in ways that bring out even more of your potential. If you already have an idea of what to do—by aren't doing it—let the book move you into action.

Over the past 10 years, my clients have tested the strategies of *The Naked Desk*—and they've worked. The chapters are supported by stories about real people who've faced the same hurtles you do and found a "better way." For example, you'll read Samantha's story in Chapter 1: *Organize Your Office—10 Simple Steps to Optimize Your Space and Get Rid of Clutter*. You'll unveil how she dug her way out of piles of paper, lost documents and embarrassment. About how one day she got so fed up that she took on the challenge to organize like never before. Maybe you will smile when you see yourself in the book's stories. Let them inspire hope no matter what your personal starting point is.

Read the words of this book, but more important: take action! Apply at least one step—any step—each day. Build on your progress. Know that you **can**. With a little momentum, you'll experience greater energy and ease with less stress as you build a richer, more meaningful life. You'll have everything you need to establish the way of *The Naked Desk*.

It's your time. It's your life. Turn the page and let's go!

Sue Brenner
Santa Cruz, California

chapter [1]

Organize Your Office

10 Simple Steps to Optimize Your Space and Get Rid of Clutter

FIVE MINUTES before the seminar began, Samantha whispered to her co-leader Scott, "Oh no! I forgot the handouts for the participants!"

"Give me your keys. I'll run to your office and get them." Scott grabbed Samantha's keys and ran out the door. Samantha looked out at the audience. One minute till show time. Fear gripped Samantha and she began to sweat. But not about starting the seminar without Scott. Instead, she found herself thinking, *"He's going to see the mess in my office!"* And it was no ordinary mess. Stacks of papers, piles of books, plates, suit jackets, coffee mugs. Clutter everywhere. Samantha shuddered, but turned on a smile for the group. With a deep breath, she introduced the seminar.

Meanwhile, back at Samantha's office, Scott snorkeled through a sea of papers for 20 minutes until the handouts bubbled to the surface. He rushed back to the seminar, now 40 minutes later. "Samantha, why can't you get it together?" he thought.

Samantha could barely face him at the break. Her heart pounded. "Scott, I'm so sorry I let you down." Scott sighed and looked away, thinking, "This isn't the first time...." Samantha continued, "I'm so embarrassed. I *know* I need to get organized."

Samantha walked outside for some fresh air. "It's not just the handouts," she thought. "I'm always late. I don't have any free time. I can't find anything. This has got to stop."

The next day Samantha arrived five minutes early to work. "Wow," Scott thought. "This is a first." She decided to finally face the mess in her office. Actually *look* at it, rather than skating over it. The organization CD she'd purchased six months ago would now serve its purpose. She played it in her car and office for the next three weeks. She listened to it over and over. And, this time, she applied the steps. Decluttering became her personal mission. Her boss provided input. She got great tips from co-workers, including Scott, who already led frenzy-free lives.

For the first time, Samantha cleared her desktop. And she cleared it again the next day. Her problems of losing important documents and forgetting things for meetings began to wane. She no longer felt out of control and gained a newfound sense of ease she'd never felt before.

How did she do it? Here are some of the steps Samantha used. You too can experience less stress, peace of mind, and more productive work days.

Step 1: Look at the Forest First

Stand in the doorway of your office right now. What do you see? Take in the big picture. Before you get distracted by each "twig" scattered around, look at the forest of your office first.

Ask yourself: *What do I want to accomplish in this space?*

What do you use the space for? Do you want a beautiful space where you can find things when you need them? Do you want a simple set-up to make work easy? Do you want your desktop to be clear? Do you want a quiet, closed-off sanctuary?

Decide what's important to you. Design around that. Then your organizing efforts will go toward the ideal office you're trying to create.

For example, Dan, a business owner, chose the smallest office available. He had his desk built into the wall and removed the chair.

Why? He asked himself: *What do I want to accomplish in this space?* His answer was to connect with customers and close deals. So he didn't want to sit. He wanted to be energized and on his feet. He wanted every surface to be clutter free. And, to stay in action, he printed motivational quotes to put on the walls. He designed around these ideals to be at his best.

For your own office or cubicle, consider what you do in that space and what you want to accomplish. You can design it to be highly motivational, serene or a place that allows you to concentrate—it all depends on what work you do and what kind of environment will help you function at your best.

> **TIP:** Don't skip this "big-picture" step. Especially if you're new to organizing and want it to last, take a step back and see the forest first. Know what you want before you take action.

Step 2: Examine Your Stuff

Look at the stuff in your office. Become aware of how much you've accumulated.

> **TIP:** Make yourself examine each and every thing. Even if you have to pick each item up to get a closer look.

What do you need? What's in the way? Professional organizer, Andrea Robinson, offers three questions to ask about every item you've stored in your office: (1) Does it have a home? (2) Does it need a home? (3) Does it need to leave?

Assess the layers of clutter to uncover what's important and what's not.

> **TIP:** If you tend to keep everything, ask someone else: "Does this item need to go?" A neutral person will be better able to tell you what you need to toss. Be sure you ask an analytical person, not a sentimental one.

Step 3: Take the Purge Test

OK. You've examined your stuff. You've found some things that need to leave. You've found some things you're not sure about. To clear out your space further, it's time to take the purge test.

Look at an item you're not sure whether to keep or pitch. Ask these questions to get clear:

✓   Do I use it?

✓   When is the last time I used it?

✓   Do I need it?

✓   Does it make me more productive?

✓   Do I have more than one of this item?

✓   How many of this item do I need?

✓   Does it bring me joy?

✓   Is it broken, damaged or inoperable?

✓   Would I move it from office to office five times?

✓   If I lost it in a fire, would I replace it?

✓   Is this information available on the Internet?

> **TIP:** Are you really going to fix broken items? If not, pass them on to someone who will, recycle them, or trash them.

Start to recognize why you keep things. Don't just organize—let go before you organize. Awareness is an important step.

> **TIP:** Get rid of more than you think you need to. Trust that if you need something again in the future that you'll have the resources to get it.

Step 4: Break Your Organization Projects Into Doable Tasks

When it comes time to organize, do you feel overwhelmed? Does it seem like an insurmountable task? Make it easier on yourself—something you *can* do.

Start by remembering your answer to the question: *What do I want to accomplish in this space?*

Cameron, an entrepreneur, responded with "Clients visit my office daily, so it needs to be clean and professional. I want all surfaces to be clear and I want to know where everything is so I never have to scramble for anything."

From there, he organized his office around this goal. How? By breaking the organization effort into smaller, doable tasks.

Think about the main sections of your office that you plan to organize. For example:

- ✓ Desktop
- ✓ Bookshelf
- ✓ Trash/Recycling Area
- ✓ File Cabinets
- ✓ In/Out Box
- ✓ Walls
- ✓ Door
- ✓ Table

Then look at each office section on your list and break each one into a series of tasks. Your list will provide a map to tackle each area, one at a time.

TIP: Write or type the tasks for organizing each main section of office. You'll be much more likely to do them if you put them in writing!

For example, the tasks associated with the "Desktop" area of your office might include these steps:

- ✓ Get rid of unnecessary papers.

- ✓ File documents that need to be kept.

- ✓ Put projects in folders or store them on the computer desktop.

- ✓ Remove all mugs and dishes.

- ✓ Transfer sticky note information to Outlook.

- ✓ Hang written goals on wall.

- ✓ Transfer business cards into contacts on Outlook.

- ✓ Throw dead flowers away.

- ✓ Hang headset on a hook next to phone.

- ✓ Put office supplies in top drawer—e.g., stapler, sticky notepads, and paper clips.

This way, whether you decide to tackle the whole organization in one day or break the job up over a series of days, you'll have specific steps on how to get there for each section of your office.

Stop reading now and develop your list organizing tasks for each section of your office. This will accelerate the work when it's time to implement.

Step 5: Take Action

Have you developed a plan for cleaning up your office before? Did it get swept away in the clutter? Did you fail to take action? Without action, your plan will wind up on top of the volcano-sized pile—part of the problem instead of the solution.

Climb out of the inaction hole!

Review the doable tasks you listed for each section of your office in Step 4. Schedule a time when you're going to organize. And then do it! Here are some tips.

Begin with small daily steps taken straight from your doable tasks list. Block off time in your organizer. Write it in now—30 minutes per day for one week. Then stick to it. Make sure that those around you know that you've blocked out this time to tackle the clutter. You could even enlist their help!

For example, you've decided to create a naked desk. A desk that frees your mind, sharpens your focus and sparks creativity. To clear your desk in small steps, spread your strategy list over five days. On Monday, throw away dead flowers and file necessary documents. On Tuesday, get rid of all unnecessary paper and remove any mugs and dishes. Keep going, doing a task or two each day, until your desktop is bare.

> **TIP:** If you have limited time to organize, ask yourself, "What single action would make the greatest impact right now?" Or, "What can I do in five minutes that will make the biggest difference?" Scan the office and choose the area that is calling out for order the most. Then take action!

Don't fall into the trap of organizing your clutter. The purge test in Step 3 can help you decide if something is worth taking the time to organize, or if it needs to leave. Make sure your daily steps remain visible. Print out your schedule or keep it open on your computer desktop. Once you've built some momentum, dedicate a larger chunk of time to organizing—schedule one to three hours to focus on the next section on your office organizing list.

In many cases, you can reorganize and declutter your whole office in one day. It takes dedication, commitment, and focus. But it can be done. Better yet, why not schedule a Saturday to organize your office? Then you'll arrive on Monday to a beautiful, newly decluttered space. And you'll be able to get more work done in less time when you can find what you need when you need it.

Step 6: Create a Place for Each Thing

"You can't have everything. Where would you put it?"

—Steven Wright

Samantha used to walk into her office and put her things down. Wherever. Without thinking. No wonder she couldn't find things when she needed them. So, as you take action to organize, find a home for everything.

Ask yourself: *What makes sense to put where? What similar items can I group together?*

You may need to purchase a new file cabinet or more storage bins. Find the cabinets, shelves and containers that will work best for you. Make it fun, or stylish or just practical! Whichever approach you choose, be sure to create a place for each thing and put each thing in its place.

Ask yourself: *Where will I find this?*

Then, of course, you need to remember where everything goes. The key? Instead of asking yourself, "Where should I *put* this?" ask, "Where will I *find* this?"

Give yourself time to think about where you'll *look* for something when you need it. By making this mental change, Samantha finds things quickly now!

If you put things where you're likely to look for them, then even if you momentarily forget where something is, you should be able to *figure out* where it is. By using logic up front to think about where you'll find things, it will be easier to locate things in the moment when you need them..

> **TIP:** If you stash things away because you need to clear clutter fast, go back and put these things where they belong later that same day. Stashing leads to "I can't find it." *Take the time to return things to where you'll find them*

Keep a very important documents file.

Just as she started getting the swing of the "organization thing," Samantha had a setback. Packed and ready to go, she couldn't find her passport for an upcoming business trip. It wasn't in her file cabinet; it wasn't under her desk. She'd lost this crucial document. Having learned her lesson the hard way, Samantha created a folder for important documents. Now she stores itineraries, a copy of her passport (the real deal goes in the "important documents" file at home), and a list of her user names and passwords in a "Very Important Documents" file.

> **TIP:** Shred important documents when tossing them out.

Don't miss an important business opportunity because you aren't keeping your significant documents in order. This system will prevent you from having to order new documents or from losing them all together.

> **TIP:** Important things go in well-marked special places for easy retrieval.

Step 7: Simplify

> *"It is a simple task to make things complex, but a complex task to make them simple."*
>
> —Meyer's Law

Take the opportunity to simplify at work and at home. Store experiences and memories in your heart, not in file cabinets. Pare down mementos to fit into a single box or one small area in your office, like a shelf or the corner of your desk. The best way to begin to establish a sense of order is to create *space*.

> **TIP:** Photograph it. If you're having a tough time letting go of something that you no longer need, take a picture of it. You'll still have the memory, but it will take up a lot less space!

Do you have more things than you need? Pass extra stuff along to friends or charitable organizations. Experience how freeing it feels to get rid of it. For example, look at your bookshelf at work. How many books have you read? Which ones aren't needed for the core of your job? How about passing these on to colleagues? Why not take one to your next department meeting and pass it along?

> **TIP:** Donate your unused business books to the local university or public library.

Sell items that you're not using at sites like www.ebay.com or www.craigslist.com.

Step 8: Use the 3-Bag Approach

This single technique wildly improved Samantha's ability to organize. In fact, it answered her most basic question: "I want to get organized, but *how* do I do it?" It's a fast and effective method to help you to simplify, get rid of things and pass things on.

Place three bags in the space you plan to organize. Each one will serve a different purpose.

Bag 1 – Doesn't Belong Here

Label the first bag, "Doesn't Belong Here." In this bag, collect the mugs, books, supplies and other things that don't belong there. At the end of your organizing session, go around the office to put these things back where they belong.

Bag 2 – Give Away/Return

Label the second bag "Give Away/Return." When you stumble across a report borrowed from a co-worker or things you want to give away, put them in this bag.

Surprise people by returning their forgotten books or that tie you borrowed five years ago when you forgot to pack one for your business trip! Get rid of the other items by taking them to a favorite charity as soon as you've finished the project.

Don't let the give-away bag sit in your office for six months. If you know you won't get to the charity office, many charities will pick up items for you. Or delegate to someone else to do the drop off. Immediately.

> **TIP:** When you receive gifts that you haven't used, wrap and "re-gift" them to someone else.

Bag 3 – Storage.

Label the third bag "Storage." Unless you work in a law firm or real estate office, you probably only need 20% of your papers. You can often store or access things electronically. Check with an office administrator for your company policy.

> **TIP:** Don't overstuff your storage bag. Only store important things.

To get started, scan your office. First, find an item that you know what to do with. Put it in one of your three sorting bags. Then go from there. It's also a good idea to spread your stuff out. Separate piles so that you can sift through them and see what's there.

Set a timer. Wrap up your organizing when the dinger sounds.

> **TIP:** Don't forget the trash bag! When you find something that doesn't belong in any of the three bags, throw it out!

Step 9: Embrace Your Trash Bin

Your trash and recycling bins are there for a reason. Use them! If you're wondering if you should get rid of that plastic name tag holder that you so fondly remember from your meeting with Bill Gates, yes, get rid of it. Collect all of the empty water bottles, paper coffee cups, and out-of-date papers to recycle.

Put a trash bag in your car as well. Clear out your car before the trash makes its way to your office. Don't carry your trash around from place to place.

> **TIP:** Search the net for computer recycling programs. Or put old electronic items on auction sites such as www.ebay.com.

Step 10: Capture To-Do's as You Go to Stay Focused

While you're in the process of getting organized, you may find yourself wanting to answer the phone, dash off to meet with a colleague or check e-mail. Resist all distractions! Instead, use a piece of paper or your PDA to jot down your to-dos and other ideas as you think of them. Stay focused. Rather than compulsively acting on something that will take you off track, capture it and save it for later.

> **TIP:** Set a timer. Barricade yourself in your office during your organizing time. Don't leave at all until the timer dings.

Staying Organized as a Way of Life

Find reasons to organize.

Why don't you organize? What's in the way right now? You may say, "It takes too much time." "I have more important things to do." "I'm too busy." Think about what keeps you from getting organized. Then think about the long-term consequences for your career, your stress levels, and your happiness if you don't get organized.

Then tap into the short-term and long-term benefits from getting organized. Picture your office free of clutter and imagine how much easier it will be to work in that environment. See the serene you working productively in your new space.

> **TIP:** If you don't have a compelling reason to get organized, you won't make it happen. Envision what you'll get out of being organized. Write it down and refer to it whenever you feel bogged down. Imagine the energy you'll gain without all that stuff in your way.

Make organizing a regular thing.

Don't allow your organization efforts to fall away after one or two sessions. Build in organization daily and weekly to make organization a permanent part of your work life. "Space management and time management go hand-in-hand," says professional organizer Robinson, "because all that you do to maintain your space requires time." Even if you take just five minutes at the end of each day to clear your desk, you'll experience the difference.

> **TIP:** Find 5- to 10-minute pockets of time for spontaneous organizing!

Get help.

You can apply the techniques from this book on your own. But if you simply can't face it or don't know what step you can apply today to clear out your space and get rid of clutter, ask for assistance. A Professional Organizer (http://www.napo.net) can design a road map and help you implement a plan.

You can also hire a coach to provide new tips and to keep you accountable. Or outsource parts of the organization projects by asking a few co-workers to lend a hand. The important thing is to begin the process. Then you can complete your organizing tasks, one at a time, until your office works for you.

Apply the action steps.

If you've taken even a few of the steps in this chapter—such as examining your stuff, breaking up projects into doable tasks, and using the 3-Bag Approach to organize—you'll start to notice much more ease, energy, satisfaction and productivity at work.

What's Next?

Now that you're on track with creating order and freeing up your space, you're ready to reclaim your time. Use the proven strategies in the next chapter to take back your time and use it on what matters most. When you reclaim your time, you reclaim your life.

chapter [2]

Time Is Your Life

10 Strategies to Save Time and Gain Life

But dost thou love life, then do not squander time, for that is the stuff life is made of.

—Benjamin Franklin, *The Way to Wealth*

IS YOUR SCHEDULE JAM-PACKED? Is your day overloaded with meetings, managing your business, planning and day-to-day work? Does your time get whittled away by things that aren't important to you? Do you get to the end of the day and wonder what you really accomplished? Is your work day overflowing into your home life? Do you want to grow your business even more, but can't imagine how you can fit in one more thing?

Do you wish you could—once and for all—get a handle on time so you could run your life rather than your life running you?

You're not alone. Time Management seminars, experts and books abound because time escapes people and is all too often spent on things that don't matter. Don't let the march of time spin you into a tizzy of stress and desperation. Allow time to expand to include what's most important to you.

Read Valerie's story to find out how a busy professional just like you forged room in her hectic schedule. Then apply the simple strategies to discover how to get time to work for you rather than you working for it. You'll experience greater satisfaction on the job, and in your life overall!

Success Story: Meet Valerie

Valerie wrestled with time. She poured it into her consulting business, but it still escaped her. Exhausted at the end of the day, her to-do list went on and on. To regain some time—and sanity—she asked for the help of a business coach.

Her coach asked a pointed question, "What do you want to take off of your plate?"

"What?" Valerie thought. "I'm not getting rid of anything!"

Like most people, she could not imagine removing anything from her bustling work life. She needed an outside reality check.

After reconsidering the question, Valerie realized there were many meetings each week that she didn't need to attend. She decided to have someone else lead them. Not only did this free up her schedule, it also gave her a chance to delegate and build her staff's leadership skills.

Valerie got excited by this first step. She began to discover more ways she could rearrange her schedule to free up time. The immediate positive results of forgoing those meetings led her to take on other time-saving strategies. In three months, she had freed up ten hours of "new" time per week. She began to relax more. She started exercising and her family got to see her during daylight hours.

Did Valerie's consulting business suffer? Far from it. On the contrary, her business accelerated by 60%. Why? Because by using her new time to focus on her top priorities, Valerie was able to give more focused energy to her business. You can too.

Read through all of the strategies. Highlight the three or four that will help you the most. Then put these items into action. You'll experience the reward of finding time for what matters.

Strategy 1: Prioritize—Put Your Rocks in First

In order to better manage your time, you must first know what's most important to you. Identify your top priorities right now. Then fill your day with these priorities

What's most important to you? Building your business? Getting a promotion? Leaving work at 5 p.m.? You need to focus on your priorities—the things that matter the most to you.

Here's a story that helps illustrate *how* to dedicate most of your time to your priorities.

Filling the Pail

Imagine a yellow beach pail. (Or, if you live near a the ocean, grab a bucket and actually head to the beach!)

Either literally or imaginatively, fill your bucket with as many *rocks* as you can.

Does the bucket look full? Yes. But the gaps between rocks can be filled up. So you drop some *pebbles* into the pail to fill the spaces between the rocks.

Now the pail spills over with rocks and pebbles. But there's still room for something else—*sand*. Pour sand into your bucket. Watch it glide over the rocks and pebbles as it fills in the crevices.

Surely the pail is full now. But, no. Pour *water* into the bucket and watch as it sinks to the bottom, finding its way among the sand, pebbles and rocks.

The point of this story? If you think it's to cram as much as possible into the pail, guess again. The real point is to put the rocks in first. Your rocks. The "big" things that are most important to you. If you don't fill your pail with rocks first, pebbles, sand and water will fill all the spaces—leaving you with a sense of "lack" and the pang of dissatisfaction.

What are your rocks?

For example, Kevin, the manager at a high tech company, has these rocks:

- ✓ Maintaining good relationships with key company stakeholders. (Without them, he can't effectively move ideas and projects forward).

- ✓ Managing his department. He wants to make sure his department is focused on company priorities and producing revenue.

✓ Overseeing top projects in his department and empowering project managers to succeed.

As an effective leader, Kevin consistently schedules chunks of time for his rocks each day.

Make a list of your rocks now. Be sure to include your whole life, not just work. By fulfilling your family needs, and giving attention to your hobbies and leisure, you'll experience more satisfaction and productivity at work.

> **TIP:** Include personal rocks too— such as time off. Your personal priorities will affect how you conduct your work day.

What are your pebbles?

Kevin's consist of:

✓ Mentoring new employees.

✓ Generating new product ideas.

✓ Reviewing updates on industry competitors.

Kevin finds pockets of time around his rocks for his pebbles.

Define your pebbles now. Once you schedule your daily rocks, find spots for pebbles as well.

> **TIP:** If you ride the bus or subway to work, use that time for some of your pebbles, such as researching company competitors.

What is your sand?

Kevin's sand entails:

- ✓ Day-to-day work tasks.

- ✓ Responding to non-urgent calls, text messages and e-mails.

- ✓ Reading up on his industry.

Kevin finds pockets of time around his rocks and pebbles for his sand.

Identify your sand now. Sprinkle it into your day. Just make sure it doesn't take up your *whole* day. Stay focused on your rocks first.

> **TIP:** Group your sand activities into specific blocks of time. For example, return calls from 4:00 to 5:00 p.m.

Where is your water?

These are the unimportant and non-urgent things that easily steal your time. So why do you do them? Perhaps you don't realize that they're "empty tasks," or you do them to feel as if you're doing something—to avoid your other work and appear busy.

Kevin's water includes:

- ✓ Extended lunch meetings with colleagues with whom he already has good relationships.

- ✓ Surfing the net—starting with good intentions but drifting off.

- ✓ Watching news reports on the net. (His way to numb himself when things get stressful.)

Take a moment to think about and list your water now.

Pour your water into your day during breaks or after you've addressed rocks, pebbles and even sand first.

> **TIP:** A little water can recharge you. A lot of water can drown you.

Strategy 2: Target Your Action

Make sure that your action items line up with your priorities—the rocks you just defined. If they don't, you're spending your time on non-priorities. As in the classic quote from Lewis Carroll's *Alice in Wonderland,* unimportant "water" activities put you on a treadmill:

"My dear, here we must run as fast as we can, just to stay in place. And if you wish to go anywhere, you must run twice as fast as that."

You should have your rocks scheduled into your calendar *first.* Pick three action items only each day. Scan your vast to-do list and hone in on three rocks that you will address or accomplish today. For example:

- ✓ Work on new project.
- ✓ Contact 10 past clients.
- ✓ Have meeting with boss about promotion.

> **TIP:** Remember your top three priority tasks come straight from your *rocks.*

Go to work on these priority tasks. When you complete them then address other to-dos. Don't get side tracked by unimportant things. Learn to prioritize and stick to your list. Be honest and productive about what you *really* need to get done *now*.

For example, Paul started a new job as Director of Products at an international company. During his first month on the job, he determined that one of his rocks was to establish his credibility and reputation as a strong leader who could move his division forward. Keeping this rock in mind, he paused to assess a situation to discern his targeted action step.

"When I started I quickly found the chance to help a woman get her product launched and up to speed. It knew this could forward my career and my department. I dropped everything and organized to meet with her. I wanted hands-on details.

"I brought a pile of reading home to study the woman's product the night before our meeting. But when I got home I chose 'no.'

"I decided to have dinner with my wife and watch TV. We had a nice meal. At 11:00 p.m. my wife went to bed. Again, I thought maybe I would read. But I decided that rather than stay up reading until 2:00 a.m. that I would get up at 5 a.m. instead.

"I did so, but instead of reading the product details I used the morning time as reflection time to mentally prepare for the upcoming hour-and-a-half meeting. I asked myself: How will I manage my time with the coworker? What process will I use? What questions will I ask? I had an epiphany—I didn't need to know the content of her product. My job was to facilitate her and her process. This was so effective and powerful!

"As it turned out, I finished the meeting with her an hour sooner than I'd planned. She walked away with action steps and clear directions to turn the launch around. I saw confidence flash in her eyes.

"I worked out how to focus my time better and, as a result, conserved my energy. I figured out how to facilitate the meeting and walked out feeling energized rather than weighed down. I took on two tasks to demonstrate taking action and delivering action. But I didn't take away her work from her. I knew I didn't need to do it for her. Instead, I empowered *her* to manage the work herself."

You can see how Paul almost slipped into spending his time on the nonpriority task of reading up on his colleague's product. He caught himself though. When he took a step back, he made an effective decision to use his time at home to relax with his wife—actual quality time! Then he spent his morning time focused directly on his big rock—to build his reputation as a strong leader at the new company. He did that through *empowering* his in-trouble co-worker, not by taking over.

Consider your own work situation for a moment. If a new project has made it to the top of your priorities, dedicate blocks of focused time to it. Don't spend time chatting in the halls, answering e-mails and surfing the net during project times. Watch out for little distractions that lengthen your hours at the office. Spend the bulk of your hours on your targeted daily actions. Notice your productivity accelerate and your smile widen.

Strategy 3: Focus Your Mind First

What's your very first priority of the day? To focus your mind. Consider it your warm-up before stepping onto the field.

When you wake up, do you hit the snooze bar seven times? When you do finally get up, do you jump out of bed, gulp a cup of coffee and run out the door? How you start the morning is a reflection of how you live your life.

Instead, start your day with 15 minutes to focus your mind in solitude. It's what Paul did in the above example. And it turned his whole day around and led him to achieve results on his number-one priority. Your brain, too, will sharpen and your productivity will increase just from this one step.

> **TIP:** Pause *before* you begin.

Use this focused time to set intentions for the day. For example, "I intend to give the engineering presentation with ease and humor." Then visualize your whole day. Picture how you attend meetings, how you work on projects, how you interact with others. Imagine yourself calmly resolving problems. Sports professionals like Tiger Woods know the power of visualizing plays before the game. It works.

> **TIP:** If 15 minutes seems impossible, start with one minute a day for one week. The next week, spend two minutes each morning. You'll quickly build your endurance.

Strategy 4: Take Something Off Your Plate

OK. You've calmed your mind in the morning. You feel sharp and ready to go. Now look at your week, your month, your entire work schedule and remove something.

Use Valerie's story from the beginning of this chapter to get you motivated. She stopped going to meetings that she didn't have to attend. What can you remove? Nothing? Think again. Remove unimportant items from your plate. Eliminate what you don't personally have to do.

> **TIP:** Just because you always do it doesn't mean you should be doing it.

Here's how. Review the things you do regularly that consume too much of your time or drain you. Do you have to do them personally? Can you outsource them? Are these things important or are you just in the habit of doing them without thinking?

Do you make to-do lists and then feel bound to them? Get out of the trap of compulsive doing and focus on what's most important. Remember the priorities that you set in Strategy 1. The truth is, there are many things on your lists that are not urgent and not important. Remember the *sand* that can fill your bucket if you don't put the rocks in first? When the sand fills up your whole bucket, pour it out!

> **TIP:** Just because you're good at it doesn't mean you have to do it!

Strategy 5: Eliminate Lateness

While you're at it, there's another thing to take off your plate—being late. I can already hear groans from some readers. But keep going. There's value here.

If you chronically arrive late to meetings and appointments, what does it cost you? Do people expect you to be late? Do they think you're "flaky"? Does your stress increase as you run into a meeting late? Does lateness hold you back from opportunities and promotions? If you're OK with these consequences, then don't change the tardiness habit. But if you're tired of being late, read on.

Leave early.

Challenge yourself to leave 15 minutes before your on-site meetings start. For off-site meetings and appointments, leave 30 minutes early. Try it. It will show you that you have more time than you think. You will arrive at ease and ready to go. This alone can increase your productivity and profitability. What will you do when you arrive early? Use that extra time for things that matter—like getting focused for the meeting.

> **TIP:** Play a trick on your brain. When you're hurrying from one appointment to the next or running late for work, tell yourself, "I have plenty of time." Trick your brain into relaxing. Get off the adrenaline treadmill.

Avoid doing just one more thing.

A recipe for lateness: Do as many things as you can in the two minutes you have before you pick up your keys to leave. Contrary to the idea that you're multi-tasking and therefore using your time efficiently, doing "just one more thing" is a trap. Rather than saving you time, it escalates stress and can throw off your schedule all day. It can even extend your work day. Have a "leaving the office" or "leaving the house" deadline and stick to it.

> **TIP:** If you can't stand doing nothing before you leave, do something simple and calming, such as reading a book or taking the time to prepare mentally for the next thing you're doing. "Sand" or "water" activities are fine here. Set a timer so you don't lose track of time!

Strategy 6: Complete Something You've Been Putting Off

Shorten your to-do list. If you let things pile up, they'll rob you of time when you need it most. Get something done that's been on your list day after day. This will immediately refuel your energy and free up mental space to focus on priorities. Clear off your desk (refer to Chapter 1: *Organize Your Office*) or return a phone call. Then pause and take a moment to enjoy the satisfaction of getting things done.

> **TIP:** Take one hour this week to complete something you've been putting off.

Strategy 7: Declare Yourself Complete

Finish each day and be done with it. You have done what you could. Some blunders and absurdities no doubt crept in; forget them as soon as you can. Tomorrow is a new day; begin it well and serenely and with too high a spirit to be encumbered with your old nonsense.

—Ralph Waldo Emerson

Business consultant Tex Johnstone says this step is key. If you face the end of the day and 185 unanswered e-mails still sit in your inbox, say to yourself, "I declare myself complete." This sends a signal to your brain that you're done. Free yourself to let go and move on with the rest of your day. Your days could, and sometimes do, extend into twelve, fourteen or even more hours. Save time for the rest of your life too. You'll be happier. And more productive.

> **TIP:** Saying, "I declare myself complete" also works wonders when you're stuck in traffic, during a conflict, or when you're about to go to sleep at night. It invites the mind to release.

Strategy 8: Accept That You Can't Do It All At Once

"What? But I want to do it all!" you may say.

This one can be hard to agree to—especially if you're passionate about work and life. But remember that what you take on can take place over a period of time. It doesn't all have to occur right now.

> **TIP:** Look up from your to-do list. Take a sip of coffee. Notice the leaves turning orange on the autumn trees. Glance at a photo of your children. For a moment, realize that life expands beyond your list.

Gail was working two jobs, attending evening workshops, launching a new career, and forming a new relationship. She struggled with not having time to do the homework for a marketing course she was taking. Yet she didn't want to miss out on the opportunity to gain ideas for promoting her new business.

After some thought, she realized that not participating fully in the course really wasn't serving her. The stress she expended over the coursework that piled up weighed heavier than her financial investment in the class. Once she accepted that she couldn't do it all—at least not with quality—she dropped the class, experienced immediate relief, and freed up five hours a week.

Strategy 9: Put Back-Up Systems in Place

Once you've learned (and maybe even accepted) that you can't do it all, discover how to put back-up systems in place to save valuable time when you need it most.

Have you ever waited till the last minute to print out a document before a meeting only to discover that your printer is out of ink? Make sure you have back-up systems in place. Keep an extra ink cartridge next to your printer. Have other printers to print to if you have to. Being without reserves is not only an invitation for stress but for delays.

For example, if you take credit card orders by phone and enter them into a virtual merchant account, have the account open when receiving calls from customers. Also keep a paper copy of the credit card ordering form, in case your computer crashes one afternoon. Minimizing these delays will give you the time you need when it matters the most.

Are you giving an executive presentation? Is the Power Point projector ready to go? Have your assistant bring a backup bulb in case the projector goes out during your talk. Have a flip chart with key information and one set of handouts ready in case you get into a real jam. Keep your energy focused on the presentation, not on preventable crises.

Strategy 10: Delegate

You've saved time and decreased stress by putting back-up systems in place. Do you want to save even more time for yourself? Learn how to farm things out.

Many people, especially entrepreneurs, do a lot of work themselves. You may have a limited budget, or think that you have to do it all by yourself. You may think other people won't do as good of a job as you would. Shift that mindset. Get support! There are people out there who can do the job as well or better than you can. Be honest about your weaknesses and fill in the gaps by hiring someone who knows how to do a superior job in that area. Scattered with office work? Hire a qualified assistant to set up easy systems for you.

> **TIP:** If you already have a support team, use it. Give your staff chances to learn and succeed while you discover new pockets of time.

Be aware that you aren't good at everything. And, even if are, you still shouldn't do it all. If, that is, you want quality of life. While you may love your work, don't allow it to stretch into every corner of your existence. Remember your relationships. Your family. Your health.

> **TIP:** Start by outsourcing eight hours of work weekly to someone else.

Let go of your ego and focus on what matters most. Outsource the things that will free up your time and support you the most. Use your time to do the things you do *best* and that generate the most value or revenue for your company.

For example, if you love adding new features to the software you created because it's fun, reexamine your work priorities and assess if you really need to do it. You may be wasting time. Surely there are other programmers who are as effective as you are. What is the highest return on your time? Pitching the software upgrades to the executives (instead of adding features to the software) may be more effective in getting the product launched. From a leadership perspective, it will also increase your visibility and get you noticed.

> **TIP:** If you're a business owner, your priority is billable hours. Outsource the rest.

Success Story: Meet Mr. Delegator

Chase, an executive of an investment company, is "Mr. Delegator." It's his secret for success. How? He makes sure that he's incompetent when it comes to ordinary day-to-day work tasks. Yes, *incompetent*. He doesn't run errands. He never puts postage on an envelope. Presentations? He tells his assistant three key points, and has her craft the whole thing. How does he spend his time? On the things, and *only* on the things, that move his business forward—on the *rocks*! Finding investors. Finding new development opportunities. Closing deals. The paper is jammed in the photocopier? Don't even tell Chase—he doesn't care. He's focused on the bottom line. By being "useless" when it comes to ordinary tasks, Chase forces himself to focus on the big picture, and spends his time and talents where they are most needed..

Take These Action Steps for the Time of Your Life!

Great. You're now making progress with saving time and gaining life. Practice these time-management strategies daily for thirty days to deepen your skill. Start with three new skills to practice—such as filling your schedule with *rocks* first, taking something off your plate, and delegating. By using time well, you'll open up new opportunities for yourself at work and in life. And you'll feel happier. When you leave work at 5:00 p.m., maybe you'll even take up a new hobby or go on a date!

What's Next?

As you make progress in using your time better, you're going to need to tackle that big, heavy thing that sometimes takes even the most disciplined people off-track: procrastination. In the next chapter you'll discover why it occurs and simple ways to move past it. If you want to live a fulfilling life, you've got to look the beast of procrastination right in the eye and say, "Move over. I've got work to do!"

chapter [3]

Putting Off the "I'll Do it Later" Blues

How to Stop Procrastinating

"Never put off till tomorrow, what you can do the day after tomorrow."

—Mark Twain

DID YOU GET A GOOD LAUGH out of that quote? Or did it give you a sinking feeling because it rang too close to the truth?

Are you putting off returning client phone calls? Do you drag your feet when it comes to writing employee reviews? Are you postponing a career-defining meeting with your boss? Even though you read Chapter 1—Organize Your Office—does it seem like you'll *never* organize your office? What are you putting off right now?

What happens when you delay tasks? Do you experience energy drains? Stress? Nervousness? A sense of dread? Guilt? Sounds like you've got a case of the "I'll Do it Later" Blues.

Even if you're successful in many areas, the weight of procrastination blocks your potential. It prevents you from completing important things. It keeps you from finishing mandatory projects, focusing on actions that touch your dreams, and making money.

Ironically, when you procrastinate you still carry around those unfinished tasks in your head. Your mind and muscles constrict, zapping away vital energy.

In this chapter, you'll discover how to overcome obstacles that stall your accomplishments. You'll learn how to overcome fear and stay focused. Then you can apply these powerful techniques to reduce procrastination.

You'll develop the ability to finish what you start. You'll gain a sense of relief and freedom. You'll feel more confident and perform better.

Consider this question: What would be possible for you if you procrastinated less? What could you accomplish if you stopped procrastinating all together? It's time to change the CD and stop playing the "I'll Do it Later" Blues.

Meet Bill: A Master Procrastinator

A client of mine, Bill, dreamed about traveling the world and creating charity projects that touch the lives of children. To accomplish this, he first wanted to attain financial freedom. So he launched a home-based e-business.

Bill "thought big" in the early phases of his business. He spoke boldly at company meetings. His team backed his vision of going public with the company; they all loved the idea of retiring early! But Bill's enthusiasm usually lasted for about four hours after the meetings.

Then procrastination would sneak in. Often he found himself alone in his office with no one directing him. His unanswered phone calls piled up, his business partner's requests persisted; yet his hand resisted picking up his cell phone to call investors. Did Bill experience stress? You bet!

As CEO of the company, Bill's team relied on him and expected him to produce. They noticed when he under-delivered—he felt paralyzed from the mounting pressure. On some days, he didn't do *anything* productive. He just stared at his computer screen-saver of a tropical beach in Mexico. The more days that drifted by, the more fear gripped him.

Can you hear the fear of failure and worry that resonates in Bill's story? You'll learn how to address these procrastination instigators later in this chapter. Keep reading.

The Way Out

Here are the three keys to reducing procrastination.

Step 1: Examine what leads you to procrastinate.
Bill says: "I get these big ideas for the business and I know they can work. We have a quality product that no one else has. Then I get scared. What if people invest in my business and it fails? What if customers think the product is cool, but no one buys it? I worry about the 'what ifs.' So I turn to other activities that don't have a whole lot to do with building the business. Then I worry about not doing what I'm supposed to be doing."

Step 2: Identify how you procrastinate.

Bill says: "I procrastinate by avoiding priorities. Instead I do things I can get done fast. But I know they're not important. It's a Catch-22. I worry about not getting things done. About failing. About never making the difference that I want to make in society. So it's easier for me to do immediate tasks. I pretend I'm getting something done, anything done, rather than running off to the gym. I know if I devoted all of my worry time into my business, it would succeed. But I'm terrified."

Bill realized that worry, in response to his fear of failure, led him to procrastinate. Becoming aware of both what leads him to procrastinate and how he procrastinates enabled him to do something about it. His new awareness gave him the foundation to practice new skills.

Step 3: Practice new skills to reduce procrastination.

Because of the impact on his business and future aspirations, Bill needed to address procrastination head on. He learned and practiced the following skills. You can build them too.

Skill 1: Confront Fear

> *Your gremlin's caution about life and living is inordinate and his methods of control are overzealous. He is not merely your inner critic or simply a part of your psychological makeup. Your gremlin is not your negative thoughts—he is the source of them. He is not your less-than-positive past experiences—he uses them. He is not your fears—he taunts you with them by creating the horror movie about your future that you sometimes watch.*
>
> — Rick Carson, *Taming Your Gremlin: The Surprisingly Simple Method for Getting Out of Your Own Way*

The fear-based behaviors of procrastination lure you to avoid, worry, delay, deceive yourself and get distracted. To loosen the grip of procrastination, you must identify the core fears associated with it and confront those fears.

What happens when you're afraid to do the job before you? Fear opens the gateway to procrastination. Ignoring a project may lead you to believe that the project will go away. But don't be deceived. Whether you wait two days or two weeks, the job will be staring you down, waiting for you to return.

Many times, you may be unaware that you're operating from fear. Learn to recognize when fear takes over. Procrastination itself is a good indication that fear is present. If you can trace the fear to its source—to what you are actually afraid of—you can overcome it.

What are you really afraid of? When it comes to putting things off, fear tends to show three faces.

- ✓ Fear of Failure
- ✓ Fear of Success
- ✓ Fear of Finishing

Fear of Failure

Consider Jim, a project manager who didn't follow up with any team members during a new product project. He postponed status meetings and put off his manager when she asked for an update.

Jim could tell himself, "Of course, if I followed up with my team members the project would succeed."

But what if he had diligently contacted each "task owner" and the project still failed? His strong fear of failure on a tough project drove him to elude needed communication with the project team. In essence, Jim stopped before he even started.

> **TIP:** The ego will go to great lengths to avoid failure. But make sure you assess whether this aversion to failure is actually heading you toward what you fear most—failure!

Conquering Fear of Failure

What does it take to overcome fear of failure? What support can you get to confront your fear?

When you feel the fear of failure nipping at your heels pause and assess the situation. Ask yourself these questions:

- ✓ What do I need to do to get the job done?

- ✓ Whom can I add to my team to get a better result?

- ✓ Do I have the skills needed for the job? If not, can I gain the skills quickly, ask someone else, or add another person to the team?

- ✓ What is the *likely* outcome of the project? (Not the best case or worst case, but the *likely* case.)

Let the answers to your questions reassure you and help you identify the best next steps. Breathe easier as you move you out of fear and into confidence in what your next step will be.

> **TIP:** If you truly are in over your head, take responsibility. Ask for help or transfer the project to someone else.

Fear of Success

"The price of greatness is responsibility."

—Sir Winston Churchill

The people I coach are already successful. They are professionals—doctors, lawyers, engineers, business owners, real estate agents—who have excelled in their fields. It may surprise you that a major roadblock many of these high achievers face is *fear of success*.

Take Rhonda, for example. She worked sixty-hour weeks traveling and meeting with clients to sell lasers and other medical devices. Maintaining relationships was an essential and time-consuming part of the job. One quarter, she pushed herself extra hard to exceed her sales goal; she was up for the challenge and wanted to reap the financial rewards from sales commissions and bonuses.

Rhonda set a goal to sell $700,000 in products. By the end of June, she'd exceeded her goal by 10%, arriving at $770,000 in sales. A day later—when the thrill of the victory had worn off— fear tightened her chest. "Oh no!" She panicked. "What am I going to do now? How can I keep this up?"

The pressure intensified when her boss said, "Great job, Rhonda! I'd like to see you hit $900,000 in sales next quarter."

Fear of success, or fear of even greater success, creeps in when you realize that people may expect more from you when you excel. Or when you worry that someone else deserves the success you achieved, especially if it was a breeze to attain. The irony is that success brings consequences and changes—even if they're mostly good—that can evoke anxiety.

If you hang low, if you don't tap your potential, if you hide out and don't try, then no one will expect anything of you and you won't have to face what success brings.

But, if you confront your fear of success—and move through it—the rewards will be greater than hiding out. When you access your potential, your satisfaction soars and you get to offer your gifts and talents to the world.

Conquering Fear of Success

Do you bail out of projects right before the finish line? Do you side-step promotions and opportunities? Do you put in little effort toward your goals? If you do any of these things, you may fear success.

At the core of fear of success is the belief that if you succeed you will be unhappy, people won't like you, or you will struggle. There may also be anxiety about somehow not deserving the success you achieve. Also, once you do succeed, there is a fear that you won't have what it takes to sustain success.

While fear of failure seems logical and easy to identify, fear of success is tougher to spot because it is almost always unconscious. In reading the above questions, you now know, however, whether you have a tendency to fear success. Now that you've gained insight, you can do something about it.

Use the one or more of the following techniques to conquer your fear of success…so that you can succeed and enjoy it!

- ✓ Remove the excuses for being unsuccessful.

- ✓ Take in feedback from people who tell you that you're sabotaging your efforts or backsliding.

- ✓ Accept positive feedback too. Increase your ability to be recognized.

✓ Picture yourself being happy—success and all.

✓ Alter your all-or-nothing thinking, for example, "I can't take the promotion because I'll lose my marriage." Accepting one thing does not automatically cancel another. Think it through. Talk it over with key people involved.

✓ Take yourself with you. When you succeed you're still you! Keep your truest values intact. Do you value honesty? Then be honest, no matter how far up the ladder you climb.

✓ Give your gifts to the world. Don't hoard them. The world needs them.

✓ Know that there's nothing embarrassing about achievement and standing out. You can still be humble—and even private—while receiving recognition. Or, if you prefer, you can stand up on your chair and shout, "I did it!"

Fear of Finishing

Another insidious fear is the fear of actually getting something done, of wrapping it up—the fear of finishing. This fear can prevent you from completing projects—especially the ones that mean the most to you.

"If I talk with the director, I know I'll get the promotion. If I get the promotion, I'll switch departments. If I switch departments…" Who knows what will happen!

The third face of fear—fear of finishing—promises certainty. If you don't do anything, you never have to face what happens next. It's a psychological trick your brain plays on you, because time keeps marching forward whether you complete something or not. Here is some of the irrational thinking that fear of finishing invites:

✓ If I don't talk to the director, then I'll never have to find out what happens next—the status quo will continue.

✓ If I never enter the contest, I'll never know if I would have won or not.

✓ If I never write the book, I'll never know if it'll be published or not.

✓ If I never even apply for the position, I'll never know whether I would have made it at the job.

Angela, an office assistant, wanted to transition into a more meaningful career for her. But finding out what was out there and changing career courses brought up a lot of unknowns. "I realize I haven't accomplished much," she said. "It's comfortable and safe for me to be stuck."

What Angela is saying about fear of finishing is that it's cozy and safer right here and now in this uncomfortable work situation. Ironic? Yes. Human? You bet!

Peek into your own life. When have you thought staying where you are now is more comfortable than taking a leap of faith toward the change you desire? Where do you let the fear of finishing prevent you from trying?

Finishing is so final!

Take writing a book. When you're at the end, you've written what you've written and it's time to send it off. The cover has your name on it, right there in print for the world to see! Talk about putting yourself out there. Some people might enjoy it. Others might think you failed third grade grammar. You may receive e-mails pointing out six typos the editor missed! Being finished means submitting your work—imperfections and all—for others to see.

But isn't that true of the rest of your life? There are no guarantees. You proclaimed on your wedding day that "she's the one" and "forever, 'I do'"— right there in front of your family and friends. Does that guarantee the relationship will work out? You already know the statistics are against you, and yet you chose to take the bold step of following your heart anyway. Or say you quit your job and began a start-up company. Do you know how it's going to turn out? Of course not. But you took the leap.

Life and work take boldness. Don't let your fear of finishing—a.k.a. fear of the future—prevent you from choosing what your heart desires. Look forward to your new opportunities rather than back at regrets.

Conquering Fear of Finishing

Finish what you start, even when it's hard. Plow through. Take on one large project, such as writing a book. Once it's done, move onto the next one.

Get really clear on your heart's deepest desire. Imagine what it would be like to accomplish that goal within five years. Now imagine what it would be like if you *do not* accomplish that goal in five years. Or in ten. Or in twenty.

Use the technique in Chapter 1: *Organize Your Office* to break your projects down into doable pieces. Complete each piece of your project, for example, one chapter at a time for a book. Celebrate finishing each milestone and let your accomplishment motivate you to continue—and finish—the next milestone. Keep going until you finish the project.

Even if you're scared, do it anyway. Your life is waiting!

Skill 2: Focus

If you're going to get serious about succeeding—whether you fear it or not—you must learn to focus. Here's how.

Each day, ask yourself: If I could only accomplish three things today, what would they be? (This is the three daily priorities discipline from Chapter 3.)

Put these three things on your to-do list and go to work on them.

For example, Jose, a business consultant, has three *rocks*: consulting, sales and writing. From these rocks, he set three priorities on a Monday of his week:

- ✓ Meet with four clients for consulting sessions.

- ✓ Follow up with five potential new clients.

- ✓ Write a new draft of chapter four of his business book.

His three priorities guided what he would address throughout the day. His list gave him focus, which he built into his schedule to ensure he didn't procrastinate on those top three things.

Remember what's important on a daily, weekly, monthly and yearly basis. Let your rocks generate key tasks. The things that you focus on now will build the bridge toward your long-term goals. Focus on your top priorities. Carve out uninterrupted time to accelerate through top to-dos.

> **TIP:** Turn off the phone and close your office door. Concentrate. Focus.

Skill 3: Separate the "Musts" From the "Wants"

Your list of "things that I put off" probably includes things that you must do. If you don't do these things, there will be a negative consequence either in the short or long term. For example, Jana quit her job and decided to shift careers. Her number-one rock: find a new career direction. Therefore, her "musts" included:

- ✓ Take time daily to decide on and plan new career ideas and options.

- ✓ Research career options.

✓ Set up interviews.

If she doesn't follow through with these "musts," there will be consequences. First of all, she doesn't have a bottomless money reserve. She only has three months to find a new job or else it's back to a reporting job, which she does *not* want to do. So there is a threat to her happiness. She also realizes that there is a negative hit on her self-esteem the longer she's not working, making it that much more important to accomplish her "musts."

Which projects you're putting off jeopardize your job? Which ones prevent the kind of business growth your company needs? Which ones could lead to getting fired (or not getting hired again as a contractor) if you put them off? These represent your "must" projects—things to focus on first.

You may also find a series of tasks or projects that you'd like to do. Pick the ones that register as important but not urgent. (You'll read more about these items below.) Fit these into your schedule.

Finally, if you've procrastinated on to-dos that are not important and not urgent, let them go. Take them off the burner all together.

TIP: Eliminate distracting busy-work that takes away from priorities.

The trick is to focus on the musts first and also sprinkle in the important wants.

For example, if Bill spends four hours today making calls to possible investors, he can then get to the important-but-not-urgent things he's been putting off, such as sending e-cards to thank people for attending the last investment meeting, because it's important to maintain connection, but not immediately urgent. Keep in mind, however, that unattended important-but-not-urgent things can later become urgent if they're continually put off.

Skill 4: Do What's Urgent and Important First

Remember the wisdom of putting your rocks in first? (See Chapter 2.) From those rocks, you'll discover to-do's that are both urgent and important. (*Note:* Sometimes your rocks will also include things that are important but not urgent, as described below.)

Jose's urgent and important Monday task was the all-important billable hours. He met with four clients in his office back-to-back from 8:00 a.m. to noon. Both important and urgent, this activity brought him immediate income—a necessity to keep his business running.

Make a list of your urgent and important work activities. Circle the ones that are the highest priorities and get to work on them right away. Putting these items off in place of less urgent actions will only result in a bigger crisis later on.

Skill 5: Do What's Important but Not Urgent Next

The to-do's that stem out of your rocks and pebbles also include things that are important but not currently urgent.

If you could accomplish important but not urgent life goals, would you be happier? For example, what if you focused on your health now, before any symptoms arose? What if you organized and cleaned your office now, before clutter invited more clutter and before the dust bunnies settled in? Wouldn't this give you a sense of freedom? Of accomplishment? That sought-after sigh of relief that life is working? That you can do anything from here?

What if you responded to a problem in its infant stage? That is, before it becomes a big problem. Tap into the power of addressing the important but not urgent.

Using the example above, if you maintain your physical fitness now and on an ongoing basis—important but not urgent because you feel fine—you can more easily maintain joy and well-being in the future. Conversely, if you only address your health when it's urgent, it becomes much harder to correct problems at that stage.

TIP: Respond to the whisper, not the cry.

Take Jose's Monday priorities again. They directly lined up with what is most important to his business both in the short and long term. He included a mix of important/urgent paid client meetings, preceded by important/not urgent morning writing.

Would anything immediate have happened, other than a sense of guilt, if he didn't write the chapter on Monday? No. But Jose knew that in order to produce a new product and augment his consulting business with a book, he had to consistently dedicate time to writing.

So he dedicated two hours in the early morning for this task. He also set a deadline with his editor on when he would get the chapter to her. This created external accountability. And it worked. He got it done.

After lunch, Jose spent the afternoon from 2:00 p.m. until 4:00 p.m. on another important/not urgent activity. He contacted potential new clients he'd recently met at a conference. Like the book writing, this activity didn't strike him as urgent. But the calls were very important. As a seasoned business professional, Jose knew he needed to contact these prospects to assess their needs and see if they could benefit from his services, and to discover if they would hire him for business advice. Even though this follow-up activity was non-urgent, it was important to build the foundation for future clients to sustain his business.

Skill 6: Schedule It

By taking the time to schedule all your tasks, you free up your mind to focus and prioritize. Your calendar highlights what's important so you don't have to keep track of it in your head. Then stick to your calendar.

> **TIP:** Schedule everything, including what you *have* to do and what you *want* to do. Bring tasks alive—from client meetings to working on a business-building project (such as a book)—by putting them into your calendar.

Be sure to schedule in fun and relaxation too. The added advantage is establishing a balanced life that includes both work and personal activities— the ingredients for a happier you.

Life After Procrastination

Remember Bill's story from the beginning of this chapter? For Bill, getting tasks done effectively has led to better sleep, less worry and a sense of calm as he goes forward with his projects. As the grip of procrastination loosens, Bill feels more energized and takes more effective action to fulfill his aspirations. The less he procrastinates, the more distant procrastination becomes from his lifestyle.

When worry and fear of failure creep in, he now asks himself key questions: What do I need to do to get the job done? And, do I have the skills needed for the job? These questions help him climb down the ladder of anxiety onto calm ground. Bill has worked hard on overcoming procrastination to get to what he values most in life and work and to be able to reap the rewards of his efforts.

You, too, can revel in life after procrastination by applying what you gained from this chapter. Remember, the three keys to reducing procrastination are to (1) examine **what** leads you to procrastinate; (2) identify **how** you procrastinate; and (3) **practice new skills** to reduce procrastination—confront fear, focus, separate the musts from the wants, do what's urgent and important first, do what's important but not urgent next, and schedule your time.

Practice at least two of the above skills. For example, you'll reduce procrastination by simply focusing each day and separating the "musts" from the "wants" on your to-do list. Apply the two items you select daily for one week. Then for two weeks. Extend them into a 30-day period.

What's Next? More Procrastination Busters

You may find that you've practiced addressing the urgent and important first. You've shifted your focus to include important but not urgent things too. You've set a schedule, and you've managed to follow it most of the time. You've even confronted your fears. *But you still fall into the arms of procrastination.* If this is the case, the next chapter is for you.

Turn to Chapter 4: *The Top 5 Procrastination Traps—and What to Do About Them* to find solutions for even the toughest procrastination pitfalls.

chapter [4]

The Top 5 Procrastination Traps

—and What to Do About Them

"I CAN'T STAND IT!" Rudy said. "Since I started in the real estate business five years ago, I've gotten into some bad habits. I'm a big procrastinator."

Rudy announced this at the first of six motivational sales tele-classes. He lived up to his self-proclaimed reputation of being of a procrastinator. Rudy didn't attend a single class after that! His classmates rallied around him, making it their mission to get him on board. But despite calls from the instructor, his classmates' support, and a $400 monthly class fee charged to his credit card, Rudy still didn't show up. His business remained stagnant.

Liam, a new agent in the same class, said, "My biggest challenge is getting on the phone and calling people. I get uncomfortable and don't know what to say." But, to sell more houses, Liam set a goal of making 30 contacts per day with potential home buyers and sellers. He aimed to reach 150 people per week.

The first two weeks he accomplished five of his 30 contacts per day for an average of 25 per week—125 contacts short of his goal. "I'm a little discouraged," he said. "But I'm not going to lower my goal because I really want this." Two more weeks passed. Liam's results were even smaller—5 calls completed out of 300.

"OK, what's it going to be, Liam? Are you still committed to 150 contacts a week?" the instructor asked.

"I think I just have to do it," Liam said. "I'm keeping it at 30 contacts a day."

So the instructor discussed with him the obstacles—fear of failure and lack of focus. With some structure added to his day, Liam experienced renewed focus on his top priority—prospecting. He also identified and confronted his fear of talking with people. Assignments to practice sample scripts on what to say to people on the phone helped Liam progress.

After two more weeks, Liam came to class energized. "I made 145 contacts this week!" he announced. Out of his effort, Liam steadily generated new house listings to increase his sales. It took several weeks to get into the new habit of contacting people, but he began to consistently meet his weekly goal.

What's the difference between Rudy and Liam? Both had similar real estate goals. But one excelled, and one dropped out.

Liam effectively applied three skills to reduce procrastination from the last chapter—he confronted his fear, he focused, and he worked on the important but not urgent task of prospecting. Specifically, he followed a schedule each day of high-impact activities such as contacting prospects, and he lessened his fear of failure by practicing scripts so he wouldn't stumble on the phone.

Rudy, on the other hand, tried to focus for one day and then gave up. He sank into procrastination traps.

Have you also tried to apply the skills from the last chapter—such as confronting fear and focusing—but still seem to be spinning your wheels? Do you need more tools to turn procrastination into productivity? Are you just plain stuck?

If you answered "yes," you need to uncover your particular style (or styles) of procrastination.

Look at this list. Do you recognize yourself in any of these descriptions?

1. The Adrenaline Junky

2. The Nail Biter

3. Too Crazy Busy

4. The Perfectionist

5. The Couch Potato

Perhaps you identify with more than one of these procrastination traps—they can overlap.

Let's take a closer look at each of these traps. You'll notice as you read about them that all five procrastination traps have big "buts." The good news is that each trap also has tailored solutions that you can apply right away.

Trap 1: The Adrenaline Junky

"I could work on it now, but I work best under pressure."

In school, did you wait till the night before final exams to study? Did you put off a 15-page paper until four hours before the due date? Did you rely on the adrenaline of the final hour to get something done? You may have carried this habit into your work life.

Do you still need that extra jolt of "get it done now or else"? When you cram at the last minute your adrenaline soars, but so does your stress level. The quality of your work suffers. The tester finds errors in the code you wrote for the new software product. Typos pop up throughout the report you already turned in because you didn't have time to proofread. Or, worst of all, you miss the deadline altogether.

Then what? You face an angry customer? Your disgruntled boss confronts you? Maybe you're upset with yourself for waiting till the last minute *again* after you *told* yourself you'd do it differently this time.

Even if you still get a "pass" for last-minute work, think about what you could accomplish if you gave yourself more time and planned ahead! Consider the benefits to your health that would result from not putting your system through this.

Adrenaline Junkies love a crisis! They thrive on it—it's exciting and there's something immediate to focus on. But the negative impact on you and others involved is too great. Have you ever seen the sign: "Don't turn your lack of planning into my emergency?" Someone who was exhausted by too many Adrenaline Junkies wrote it.

Adrenaline Junkies may apologize profusely afterward, but they keep doing things at the last minute. How bad does it have to get before you try new habits? Do you need to miss out on a major account because the client won't put up with your last-minute behavior any more? Do you need to experience the disappointment of getting passed up for a promotion? Do you have to lose your job? Before you let your habit get to this point, try one or all of the solutions below.

Solutions for Adrenaline Junkies

First of all, start early. Really early. Start as soon as possible. Is your project due in three weeks? Start now. Use the following techniques to avoid the adrenaline rush you get from procrastination. Discover new ways to get the job that don't rely solely on adrenaline to get you motivated.

Tap into the now.

Find out what motivates you right now to get going on the assignment. What pleasure or fun can you add to getting something started now instead of putting it off? Reward yourself for starting now and continuing to progress each week. For example, Kathleen, a manager of an employee mentoring program, wants to get off of the adrenaline treadmill. So she rewards herself in these ways for getting projects started early:

- ✓ She takes a 15-minute tea break in the afternoon.

- ✓ She arranges with her boss to leave 10 minutes early to go to the gym.

- ✓ She treats herself to a smoothie at lunch.

With these activities to look forward to, Kathleen motivates herself into action sooner.

What would motivate you right now to get going on a project in advance? What would make it worthwhile?

Increase the pain of the last minute.

With the pain behind you, you conveniently forget how much trouble you got in when you and three co-workers had to stay overnight at the office to pull off your eleventh-hour project. You forget the silent treatment you got for two weeks afterward.

You experienced the thrill of the ride, the adrenaline "high"—your coworkers experienced the agony. But, on a physiological level, you experienced the agony too. It's likely that your heart raced, you lost sleep, your pupils dilated, and you ceased your exercise routine. Whether you felt it or not, the last minute involved pain. It's time to be responsible for your impact and take responsibility for the consequences of your procrastination. It's time to face the problem.

By taking responsibility for the ill effects your procrastination has on you and those around you, you'll begin to associate putting things off with pain not pleasure. You'll decrease the thrill of doing things in a crisis. Tapping into the pain, you'll remember: *The only way I pulled off the last deadline was by downing six cups of coffee the night before. Then I suffered from headaches for the next three days and had to take a sick day to recover.* Is it really worth it?

List your stress triggers.

What things trigger stress in you? List them.

For example, project manager Deanna realized she experiences stress from:

- ✓ Giving a presentation
- ✓ Planning a company party
- ✓ Returning phone calls

Once she realized her stressors, she became aware that she used the last-minute stress of these events to stimulate action. She decided to stop and reassess her approach.

Deanna needed to design up-front strategies for dealing with each event. Her approach included proactive tactics to increase early action and reduce stress along the way.

Now whenever she has to prepare a presentation, she obligates herself to update her boss two weeks before the speech. This forces her to prepare and do a practice run at that stage. By taking this step, Deanna lowers her anxiety about giving a presentation and therefore reduces the likelihood of her putting it off until the last minute. The added benefit? Deanna presents in a much more polished and professional manner with the extra practice.

To take the stress off planning company parties, Deanna learned to have a planning session right away with another co-worker, which gave her accountability. Then, within the first week, she would also create tasks and a planning schedule. She would then post the timeline, which "publicly" obligated her to stick to it.

Increase your own awareness about what triggers your stress. From there, you can build strategies to address the stress proactively so that you won't rely on the last minute to instigate action.

Meet your need for excitement outside of work.

Maybe you're an Adrenaline Junkie at work because you hunger adrenaline in your life. If that's the case, find opportunities to meet your adrenaline needs outside of work. Don't create stress at work just to get that adrenaline rush. That's not the place for it.

The world is full of extreme sports and challenging activities. Find one you like. Get your adrenaline "high" there. Try one of these:

- ✓ Play video games

- ✓ Go horseback riding.

- ✓ Take up rock climbing.

- ✓ Watch an action or suspense movie.

- ✓ Go swing dancing (or any kind of dancing).

- ✓ Create an at home spelling bee challenge.

- ✓ Attend a sporting event.

- ✓ Play a competitive sport (soccer, tennis or volleyball).

- ✓ Go skydiving (or hang gliding).

The point is to do high-adrenaline activities outside of work—get the need met elsewhere. Then you can feel calmer, more focused and more productive where you need to be—at work.

Trap 2: The Nail Biter

"I could work on it, but what if something goes wrong?"

"Anxiety! Worry! Fret, fret, fret!" This is the cheer of the Nail Biter. Those in this trap recite phrases like: "It'll never work." "Something will go wrong." "We're wasting our time."

The problem? When you're anxious you're thinking about the future. The present moment—the here and now—gets swept away by anxiety.

When you're worried, again you're thinking about the future. And you fear change. Fearing change will lead you to resist what needs to be done. For example, if completing a project requires you to learn a new skill, you'll put it off. See how you're resisting change?

In addition to the future, worry also leads you to focus on the past. The words "shoulda," "coulda" and "woulda" occupy your thoughts. You say things to yourself like, "If only I would have informed my boss earlier, he wouldn't be angry at me for the missed deadline." Do you hear how the emphasis is on the past?

When you approach a project from the Nail Biter Trap, your brain associates it with danger. Rather than the fight-or-flight response of the adrenaline junkie, you respond with paralysis. You freeze. Fear halts action.

That's like announcing into a megaphone, "Hey, procrastination. Come on over."

Solutions for Nail Biters

If you've fallen into the trap of a Nail Biter, when you get your next assignment notice the voice in your head that says, "It'll never work." Then pay attention to the worst-case scenario you paint. It's automatic. If you can notice it, you can do something about it.

Paint a brighter future.

You've mastered painting the worst-case scenario. Challenge yourself with learning how to paint a brighter future. Consider the best-case scenario too.

Give it some positive thought. What if everything went well? What if things went as planned? Ask yourself, "What if this goes well? What can I do to produce quality results?" When you think proactively and productively you won't need to bite your nails.

Stay in the present moment.

Accept right now that there is nothing you can do about the past. What you *can* do is learn from your mistakes and apply what you learned the next time around.

In school you were taught to not make mistakes. Mistakes were to be avoided and considered bad. At work, you do make mistakes and you will make them. Celebrate failure as an opportunity to grow. Expand beyond your current level of skill by embracing what your mistakes teach you.

Lift yourself out of dwelling on the past and the mistakes you've made. Also make sure not to dread the future. Stay in the present moment. Take each easy, logical next step of the project, and watch it unfold as procrastination disappears.

"You always pass failure on the way to success."

—Mickey Rooney

Breathe... again.

New projects at work trigger anxiety, worry and fear in the Nail Biter. This activates the reptilian part of your brain that prompts you to fight, flee or freeze. When this response kicks in, pause. Stop yourself for one moment.

Then breath. Ten times. Not one time or even two. Ten is the magic number. You want to ignite the part of your brain connected with logic, creativity, intuition and spirituality (the neocortex).

Fuel this part of your brain. It will release you from fighting an imaginary battle against a saber tooth tiger. It will help you address the situation at hand, moving you out of anxiety, worry and fear. This will lead you into greater calm and a sense of confidence.

This will allow you to be more creative and resourceful. It's a relaxed alert state that enables your mind to be sharp and moves you into action.

Tap into the power of peers.

An outside perspective can be a great help to the Nail Biter. Talk the situation over with a peer. Get a reality check. Be open to hearing which of your concerns are valid and which ones are F.E.A.R. = False Evidence Appearing Real.

Plan, then act quickly.

Nail Biters plan. And plan. And then plan some more.

Quit planning to plan! Take action. Even one small action step toward your objective will move you forward. Does it take risk? Yes. Will you fail? Maybe. But you might also succeed!

Yes, planning is important. It increases your likelihood of success. But limit the time you spend on planning. While Adrenaline Junkies usually skip planning altogether (they *love* flying by the seat of their pants), Nail Biters tend to *over plan*. Over planning equates to avoiding action. Which leads to increased fear. Which further leads to avoiding action!

Take about one-third of the project time to plan. Use the remaining two-thirds to implement. For example, due to a promotion you get to move from your cube to a corner office with a window. You estimate the move will take about fifteen hours of effort. Use five hours to plan out the move. Use the remaining ten hours to actually move. If you find yourself spending over five hours to plan this mini project, recognize that you've gone overboard. You can figure out the final details, such as where to place photos and hang pictures once you've moved into the new office.

> **TIP:** Draw the sketch before defining the details.

Use planning to move a project forward, not to bog yourself down in unnecessary detail. Do just enough planning to get the job done.

Trap 3: Too Crazy Busy

"I would do it, but I don't have time."

The super achiever of the office, the Too Crazy Busy person takes on everything.

"Will you cover for me at the convention?"—"Yes!"

"You're so good at proposals. Do you mind drafting a proposal before we work on it together?"—"Sure, no problem."

"We don't have funds for an event coordinator. Can you plan the 5,000 person company-wide beach party? —"Sure. I'd love to."

You can hear the need to please people embedded in all of these "yeses." It's the need to be involved. Compulsive doing.

Some people give you slack when you fall behind on one of your 27 projects because you're so busy. Some of them don't care. They want results on *their* project and will hound you until it's done. Pressure mounts. You get lost in the crazy shuffle of activity.

You're insanely busy. It's the ultimate excuse. It's a big stress builder too, and a way to get out of responsibility. The Too Crazy Busy Trap invites procrastination because you are too busy to get things done. And you might get passed up for more important projects because you're swamped with a thousand other things. "Don't give the number-one-priority project to Jim. He's too busy."

Solutions for Too Crazy Busy

"I don't know the key to success, but the key to failure is trying to please everybody."

—Bill Cosby

Say, "No way!"

Make friends with "No," "Not now," or "I'd love to, but I'm already committed to five other projects." Set limits on what you'll take on. Practice setting limits consistently until you build that muscle and the word "no" flows from your mouth easily. Give yourself a real choice whether to do something or not. This will help you feel more empowered to produce the results of which you're capable.

> **TIP:** "Selfish" in this case is actually self-care.

Take the 24-hour pause.

Do you find yourself automatically saying "yes" to everything? Does the word "yes" fly out of your mouth without thought? Take the 24-hour pause. When a request comes your way, say, "Let me get back to you tomorrow. I need to check a few things. Can you swing by my desk then?"

The next day, don't go running to find the requester first thing in the morning. If the person still needs your assistance, let him or her come to you.

Take the advice of a civil engineer's mom who told her son when he first started dating, "Don't be so *eager*."

With the time you've bought, answer the following questions:

✓ Do I *really* have time to do X?

✓ Do I *want* to do X? (For either personal or professional reasons)

✓ Do I have enough time to do a quality job on it? Is it my priority?

✓ Do I need to remove another activity to fit in this new one?

You have your own goals and priorities at work. Other people may also have priorities for you. When possible, choose your own priorities first. Then, when you have the time and space to help someone else out, go for it! But if you are already helping out sixteen people and neglecting your own priorities, you are putting your projects in jeopardy.

Remember that when you say "yes" to something you say "no" to something else. Become conscious of what you're saying "yes" to and what you're saying "no" to.

Answering these questions will allow you to make an informed decision. Your blood pressure will thank you. And you can go home at night before 8:00 p.m. You may even *enjoy* what you're already doing rather than adding to your load.

> **TIP:** Be quiet at meetings. When the leader asks, "Who wants to take on the company BBQ?" cast your eyes downward. Say nothing and let someone else take it on.

Trap 4: The Perfectionist

"I could finish it, but I want to make sure the whole thing is exactly right."

Rebecca had edited six of the seven articles she needed to complete for a client. Then she kept them sitting in her computer for three months. She just didn't think they had the right approach to write the last article and finish the project.

"Rebecca," the e-mail read. "Have you finished editing any of the articles for the website?"

Her client's web master preferred to post the articles one at a time, as they were finished. He wanted to make sure potential customers could access as many published articles by the company as possible.

Rebecca explained, "I was waiting to complete all seven of the articles before sending *any*." She wanted to present a completed project all at once. Letting go of the articles one at a time scared her. At the same time, she was afraid to finish the last article because it would mean letting go of the whole project. "It's funny how my brain works like that! I'm such a perfectionist!"

The "all or nothing" approach that the Perfectionist Trap ignites can paralyze you. Are you unable to finish a project because you fear it will never be perfect? Are you taking too long on a project because you want to perfect every detail before delivering the results to the customer?

Solutions for Perfectionists

Understand that no project is ever perfect—trying to attain perfection is just another way of procrastinating. Learn to know when a project is finished. Also, develop the discipline to turn in what you have when you've completed it.

Submit pieces as you go. Don't let the Perfectionist Trap stop you from delivering what you promised.

Know when "good" is "good enough."

Sometimes 80% will meet or exceed expectations. If you are a perfectionist, chances are your 80% equals someone else's 98%. Let yourself off the hook. Delve into the unknown of a project by beginning it and finishing it. Don't stand at the starting line in fear of taking the first step. Give yourself a chance to succeed by taking action.

Honor deadlines and turn in what you have. Communicate along the way and get feedback if you don't think your efforts are up to par. And, more important, *take in the feedback you receive.* Especially if it's positive! If your boss says your work is great, believe it! Perfectionists are not the best judges of your own work. Rely on other people's perspectives.

To step around the Perfectionist Trap, aim for excellence (which includes timeliness), not perfection. You'll enjoy life more and you'll still produce quality results.

> **TIP:** Practice doing one thing imperfectly each day.

For example, during an improvisational theater rehearsal, the students moved cautiously around the stage. They were trying too hard to be witty and to make up awe-inspiring stories. Their bodies were tense. Tight smiles stretched across their faces during scene work.

"Do it badly," the teacher said.

"What?" They asked, wide eyed.

"Do it badly, I said."

They got the message. As soon as the students let go of trying too hard the scene came alive. When they freely expressed themselves, without worrying about mistakes, the story started flowing. It was the best work they had done so far—work they could only accomplish by dropping their ideas of "perfect."

Like the theater students, practice having fun with your "imperfect acts." It will bring lightness into your life and teach you to criticize yourself less. Plus, you'll smile more and so will the people around you. And you'll get more done and get it done on time!

> **TIP:** An 80% perfect project that gets stalled out waiting for 100% perfection is of no use to anyone.

Set reasonable goals.

These are goals you can actually reach. If you're a Perfectionist, your goals may tend to be too detailed and too large to accomplish. For something you're working on, think of your original goal then scale it back.

Accomplish the goal in a series of stages. For example, Rebecca had agreed to write seven articles for her client. To achieve that project in stages, she could write a draft of article one, edit the article and then send it to the web master. She could repeat this approach for each article. Doing the project in small stages, with due dates assigned to each phase, will bring the project to completion faster and stop the Perfectionist Trap from occurring.

Take a look at one project you are working on right now. What stages can you break it into? At the conclusion of each stage, reward yourself and celebrate that milestone of success.

How will you reward yourself? Here are some ideas: Take a break and sit down at a park bench and read a chapter of your favorite book. Schedule a dinner date with your friend or spouse for that evening. Purchase five new iTunes you've been wanting to add to your MP3 collection.

The Perfectionist Trap will whisper: "You're not completely finished. You only deserve punishment." Don't listen. Reward yourself for each small success. You deserve it. This will bring more satisfaction both in the process of working towards the goal and finally achieving the goal itself.

> **TIP:** Enjoy the process not just the final product.

Own your strengths.

The Perfectionist Trap has you telescope in on minute imperfections. It overshadows the wealth of excellence that you produce. Even if you aced a presentation, for example, perfectionism leads you to dwell on the one word you stumbled over instead of focusing on your overall success.

To practice owning your strengths, start your day by stating to yourself ten things that are great about you. Do this right after you wake up. Silently lie in your bed and find ten personal strengths. Say them quickly to yourself in your head. Speed is imperative so that you don't become critical of yourself.

Then keep your strengths in mind throughout the day. Even when you inevitably falter (everyone does), you have your strengths to fall back on.

> **TIP:** Find at least one thing you can consistently do without criticizing yourself.

Trap 5: The Couch Potato

"I could work on it, but there are so many other things I'd rather be doing."

Thomas felt isolated in his job. Most of his co-workers had recently been relocated to another office. The ones remaining usually met with clients outside of the office. Thomas often found himself working alone.

An extrovert, Thomas missed the day-to-day interaction of working in person with his team. He experienced loneliness.

He used to find his work fun and effortless. But lately he found himself sitting in his chair for hours doing nothing. Then he'd gaze out of his office window for long stretches of time. Thomas had sunk into the Couch Potato Trap.

Do you find yourself in trap also? Usually, you're vulnerable to it during low points in business or life. The Couch Potato Trap sinks you to a state of non-doing and avoiding work. It also numbs your emotions.

This trap is muddy because once you sink into it you feel poorer. And non-doing is habit forming.

Do you feel guilty about spending hour after hour talking to your friends during work hours? Do you feel bad, then do nothing for a while and then feel worse? The price you're paying in mental energy and stress is just not worth it! While this is certainly human, aren't you tired of mindlessly browsing a website knowing full well that your year-end report is due next week?

Why the guilt over doing nothing? Because people count on you at work. Your company hired you to fulfill a certain role. Your employee pays you a wage for that role. When you spend paid hours "kicking back" you essentially steal from your employer. You also rob yourself of your own potential.

The Couch Potato Trap stalls progress as well. Any momentum you've gained on a project comes to a halt. Then it takes that much more energy to get things rolling again.

Solutions for Couch Potatoes

Use your time wisely.

Ask yourself: What's the best use of my time right now? If it's a Saturday, kicking your feet up to watch your favorite sporting event may be a good answer. But if you're logging in work hours, pick a more productive activity. Even the mundane parts of your job such as filing, rank higher than the Couch Potato items such as staring into space.

Shift your language.

"I'm lazy. It's my nature."

If you say this to yourself, you're cementing the Couch Potato Trap in place. When you see a behavior, such as laziness, as part of your identity it implies you can't do anything about it, and you're not responsible for it. But that's not true. You *can* change habits. Even long-ingrained ones.

Start by shifting your language. Instead, say, "I've acted lazy in the past, but I want to get back to work again." Notice that the phrase is in the *past tense*. By speaking and thinking in the past tense, you make the problem a *behavior* that can be changed, rather than a personality flaw that is a permanent part of who you are.

Say your new phrase out loud for seven days straight—"I've acted lazy in the past, but I want to get back to work again." Notice as you say this how it begins to shift the way you think about your behavior as separate from yourself. This will inevitably invite you to take positive action.

For example, Mira, a manager, found herself surfing the Internet for at least an hour per day. She used to think nothing could be done about it until she said to herself: "I have been lazy in the past." When she said that to herself, she immediately replied, "Wait a minute! I used to be a high producer! I was the number one producer not so long ago…" Mira tapped back into the part of herself that was Couch Potato free. The part that was, in fact, a super achiever. Then she asked herself, "What can I do today to be productive?" This prompted her to get back on track.

Once you have stated your Couch Potato behavior in the past tense for seven days, add Mira's question—What can I do today to be productive?— daily for another seven days. Notice the shift in how you think about yourself and, therefore, in how you act! Placing your Coach Potato in the past may shift you back into high gear again.

Up your motivation.

There are other questions that can lead you toward positive action as well You do have energy for the things you want to do in life. To increase your motivational juices, ask yourself these questions.

What am I doing right now? Am I wasting time? Am I "earning my keep"? For example, you may find yourself working hard to meet a deadline or doing the day-to-day work tasks. If, however, you have slipped into the Couch Potato Trap at that moment, you'll remind yourself to stop and assess your behavior. For example, if you respond with, "I've been playing with the loose thread on my coat jacket for the past thirty minutes," snap out of it. Refocus your mind and get back to work.

> **TIP:** Ask yourself this question—What am I doing right now?—throughout the day until it becomes ingrained in your subconscious and you're automatically aware of what you are doing *right now*. Soon you will stay on task without having to think about it.

What's the benefit of acting now? What benefits can you identify from getting into action right away? What are the pluses of not delaying? If you act now, for example, your workload won't pile up even more later. If you act now, you can go home at 5:00 p.m. instead of 8:00 p.m. If you act now, you can finish your project before you leave for vacation next week instead of bringing your work with you. You get the idea. Tap into the benefits of getting into to action right away and reap the many rewards.

What's important about focusing on work right now? If you answer, "nothing," you are caught up in the Couch Potato Trap, and you are deceiving yourself. Self-deception limits growth and hampers you from meeting your potential. Ask again. Possible answers are listed here:

- ✓ Because I'm up for the challenge.

- ✓ Because I want to be the first one to complete this report.

- ✓ Because otherwise I will really get off track.

- ✓ Because other people are relying on me.

- ✓ Because that's what I'm being paid to do.

- ✓ Because my boss will notice and my job depends on it.

- ✓ Because I'm already on probation and can't afford to lose my job.

Who do I want to become? The action you take today shapes your behaviors and leads to the person you will become. Most of you have an inkling of your ideal self. You may find that you want to be one or more of the following:

- ✓ Motivated
- ✓ On track
- ✓ A "can do" person
- ✓ Your personal best
- ✓ Competent
- ✓ Well-liked
- ✓ Contributing
- ✓ A provider for your family
- ✓ Your own definition of a "good person"

To develop these qualities, back away from the Couch Potato Trap and take conscious, decisive action.

Get interested ...or even excited!

Think about what attracted you to your job in the first place. Tap back into the interesting parts of your job. Find ways to enjoy work again.

Refresh your outlook on your job. Reengage with it. Keep your focus to rediscover excitement. Make work fun again. For example, conflict between his boss and his department had worn down Mike, the director of a telecommunications company. He'd slipped into the Couch Potato Trap, which numbed his anger. By closing his door, he avoided hours of work and made it appear that he was busy.

Used to being a contributing team player, Mike soon got bored with his inaction. To reengage with work and get recommitted, he thought back to what interested him most about his job. It was developing people. So he put extra time into each employee review. Then he provided thorough feedback to each of his team members to set each of them up for success as they progressed in the company. This action did it for Mike. He got back to his enthusiastic, high-performing self by remembering what excited him about his work.

Get fit.

Exercise can do wonders for motivating you in many areas of your life. A fit body and sharp mind keeps the Couch Potato Trap at bay.

For increased accountability, hire a personal trainer. That way it hurts your pocketbook if you don't show up. A great motivator!

Catch it early.

You've discovered many solutions to overcome the Couch Potato Trap. When you fall into this trap and do-nothingness gets you off track, choose to get back on track as soon as possible. Don't let laziness induce more laziness. Catch it early. Get into action. Ask yourself those four questions you've learned (and answer them) to get yourself back on track:

✓   What am I doing right now?

✓   What is the benefit of acting now?

✓   What is important about focusing on work right now?

✓   Who do I want to become?

> **TIP:** Ask yourself these four questions over and over throughout the day. Do this until they become ingrained in your subconscious and you no longer have to think about them.

Action Beats Procrastination!

Once you've identified the Procrastination Trap(s) you fall into, apply one or more of the solutions for that trap consistently each day. Take action. Take any action. Keep going and you will experience rewards at work that include greater happiness, better results, less stress, and more ease without the weight of procrastination looming. These benefits will ripple through to all areas of your life.

What's Next?

"But wait! I still don't have a grasp on getting over procrastination," you may say. Why? There are other traps that may still be lurking. In the next chapter, you'll discover four more hidden procrastination traps that you may fall into. These traps—Pie-in-the-Sky, It's Beneath Me, You Can't Make Me, and The Self-Indulger—work just as hard to keep you down as the top five traps do! So read on to find more solutions to those slippery procrastination traps and to uncover effective solutions you can apply to get rid of them.

chapter [5]

More Hidden Procrastination Traps

—and How to Overcome Them

HAVE YOU SLID PAST the Top 5 Procrastination Traps? Are your procrastination pitfalls harder to identify? Tell yourself the hard truth as you answer the following questions:

- ✓ Do you daydream about big ideas that you rarely implement?

- ✓ Do you view parts of your job as "beneath you," so you put them off?

- ✓ Do you fight certain projects, saying to yourself or your boss, "You can't make me do it"?

- ✓ Do you spend time on things that produce immediate pleasure, like steaming milk at the hot chocolate machine, instead of getting down to business?

If you responded with a "yes" to any of these questions, then one (or more) of the Hidden Procrastination Traps has captured you:

1. Pie-in-the-Sky

2. It's Beneath Me

3. You Can't Make Me

4. The Self-Indulger

As with the Top 5 Procrastination Traps, these extra four also have big "buts." Read on to find out how to overcome them.

Hidden Trap 1: Pie-in-the-Sky

"I could work on it, but the idea of it is more appealing than actually doing it."

> *"He lay beside her, an insomniac with visions of vastness. He thought of desert stretches so huge no Chosen People could cross them. He counted grains of sand like sheep and knew his job would last forever. He thought of aeroplane views of wheatlands so high he couldn't see which way the wind was bending the stalks. Arctic territories and sledtrack distances. Miles he would never cover because he could never abandon this bed."*
>
> —Leonard Cohen, *The Favourite Game*

Imagine that you're in charge of planning an off-site sales meeting. Some of you might think about a picnic on the beach for the meeting. If you fall into the Pie-in-the-Sky Trap, however, you think the beach meeting idea is too small—anyone could do that! You feel compelled to think bigger!

But Pie-in-the-Skyers think beyond BIG. Instead of a simple activity for the meeting, you think of simulated moon launches and African safaris. You can't wait to see the sales force brimming with motivation atop an elephant ride in the jungle. Budget and the time required for this epic meeting don't cross your mind. You just create a grand scheme for what the company *could* do.

Instead of throwing down a few rocks to cross a stream you want to build the Golden Gate Bridge.

Your creativity and passion are strengths. But does your idea match what the company or customer wants? Calling events exciting names and thinking big isn't necessarily going to get the job done. In fact, the Pie-in-the-Sky Trap can get in the way of accomplishing a result.

For example, Jacob started a new position managing the marketing department of a high tech company. Excited about what was possible for the company, Jacob latched onto one product—a piece of software to assist clients with day-to-day efficiency. Though several products of its kind already existed in the marketplace, Jacob envisioned creating a web-based tool that combined the bells and whistles of every hot piece of software he could think of.

His passionate presentation at the leadership meeting got him buy-in for the project. He received needed funding and started putting in 14-hour days to develop the software.

The features of the software kept growing and expanding. Every week, Jacob thought of new things to add. Soon he had to request more money.

He was so enthusiastic about the product that he began to advertise it to customers before it was finished. His clients added other ideas, which further expanded the scope.

When a co-worker shyly suggested that a similar product existed, but that it was much simpler and would be easy to replicate, he balked. To Jacob, simple was boring. He figuratively wanted to re-invent the wheel with added lights, new spokes and aerodynamics.

Deadline after deadline passed. The budget inflated. Countless work hours mounted from designers, developers and engineers.

The executive sponsor finally called STOP! He cancelled the project all together.

Within a month, Jacob the marketing manager submitted his resignation. Because most of his focus had gone toward the software development, he did not meet his marketing and sales objectives. And this meant his position at the company was vulnerable. He opted to bow out before they asked him to leave.

Although Jacob talked a great story and stirred possibility in people's minds, in the end he didn't deliver.

Like Jacob, when you make things more complex than they need to be, you experience over-extended schedules, stress and inflated budgets. Not to mention disgruntled workers and all-around fatigue. Some ideas are so outlandish, in fact, that they never get off the ground. You become overwhelmed by your own vision.

> *"Vision without action doesn't amount to a whole hill of beans."*
>
> —Karen Kimsey-House, Founder: The Coaches Training Institute

Pie-in-the-sky visions of grandeur can apply to one massive project or to several smaller projects that demand resources. Going overboard in the design of a project can lead to the predicament that Jacob faced: the project never gets done.

Some of your visions may be so huge that you never move out of idea mode. In essence, you stop yourself before you even start. By focusing more on the design than the implementation you effectively procrastinate and avoid the "doing" part of the project indefinitely.

Solutions for Pie-in-the-Skyers

Use your big thinking ideas for strategic planning meetings and building your company's or department's vision. That's where they belong. Rather than impulsively throwing out one grand idea after another, submit your ideas to the decision makers in the company.

For example, Rico, the "idea guy" and VP of a large consumer gift product corporation, tossed out ideas for new products every day. People liked his ideas. They were innovative and fun. And Rico never had a shortage of them.

The problem arose when he'd walk by a person's desk at random and say: "Here's my idea for a new product. Get working on it."

With such a flurry of ideas, very few of them got done. Just as a person started one project, Rico sent another one that person's way. People felt overwhelmed, and confusion swept through the product development department.

The other executives didn't want to dampen Rico's idea generation. They relied on him for innovating new products to sell. However, with the tightening economy, the company could no longer afford to throw money and resources at every idea Rico had.

A two-part solution emerged. You can use it too.

Create an Idea Box.

The design department made an Idea Box for Rico. He placed it on his desk. Every time a wild idea came to him, he'd jot it down and put it in the box. This satisfied his need to create ideas.

You entrepreneurs you can also create an idea box inside a folder on your computer. When you think of an idea, type it and tuck it away. Realize that you don't have to act on every idea today. Review them a week or a month later and discern which ideas you want to build further.

Create your own Idea Box. Create a fancy box, a bowl, a cork board with colored post-its, or a computer folder so your ideas have a place to go.

Find the "keepers."

The executive team (decision makers) would periodically review Rico's ideas and decide which ones to bring to market. This gave the employees focus and direction. Projects started moving again and got done! Rather than firing Rico, the company redirected his energy and channeled his innovation skills in more effective and purposeful ways.

When an idea gets selected, your company will dedicate resources to it. Create a set of three criteria to help you decide which ideas to develop further.

Rico's story shows what to do if you come up with idea after idea. Then, for ideas that are selected, it's important to know what the goal of each idea (or project) is.

Rein in your projects.

For each idea that becomes a project ask: What is to be accomplished, and by when?

As with organizing your office, break it down to doable tasks. Then, most important for Pie-in-the-Skyers, *stay within the scope of this goal*.

If the goal reads, "To install a new phone system by July 20, 2007," keep it at that. Unless the customer requests otherwise, don't expand it to a larger undertaking such as, "To install a new phone system and computer network."

If you want to extend beyond the original scope, talk with the stakeholders and other decision makers about it. Widening the scope of a project often entails a larger budget, more resources and lapsed schedules, so it's important to make sure that the sponsors want a bigger scope. Using their input can assist you with keeping the project realistic and allows you to focus on getting the project done rather than pie-in-the-sky ideals.

Recognize whether the end-goal requires a mega billboard or just a pocket-sized snap shot. Get the "doers" on board for the implementation. Create your own Idea Box. Put your lofty ideas there. Pull them out for your company's planning sessions and focus on the ones that line up with your company's values and goals. Leave the ones that don't get picked up in the box to germinate or die off, as the case may be. Don't distract yourself with pie-in-the-sky ideas that aren't in alignment with the company's goals.

Hidden Trap 2: It's Beneath Me

"I could do it, but I shouldn't have to."

Do you have a coworker that is "above" certain tasks and refuses to do them? Or is that you? Is it tough for you to "lower" yourself to do certain things, even if they're part of your job?

Perhaps you feel that, due to your experience, you shouldn't have to do certain things. That's up to you and your boss to negotiate. Or, as a small business owner, you may decide that filing is a waste of your time. Fine.

Delegate it to someone else. But don't have it be another thing that you put off.

What about the parts of your job that you perceive as "beneath" you yet still have to do? Procrastinating will not make them go away.

Take Nigel, VP of Technology, for example. A large portion of his job requires him to sell photocopiers directly to his customers. The company's revenue depends on it. Getting the salary Nigel desires also depends on sales generation. Meanwhile, he has become exceptional at hooking up copiers to the network to allow printing from the computer desktop. As a master of this technology, he begins to feel "above" calling customers, especially if it requires him to cold call new customers. *Why should I have to do that?* So he outsources some of the work to a sales assistant and drops the rest.

Nigel was able to ride along for a while without calling customers, masterfully implementing one stellar system after another. But eventually the phone stopped ringing. E-mails ceased. His sales had run out with his existing customers and he hadn't been getting any new ones.

Solutions for "It's Beneath Me"

Humble yourself.

To win the sales game again, Nigel realized he had to get back in it. At a sales meeting, he told his story: "I've gotten complacent. I have to discipline myself to pick up the phone again."

He did. He poured admirable discipline into contacting customers regularly. He "humbled" himself to make the calls and send the e-mails. His customers were glad to hear from him. They upgraded their machines and purchased additional products.

It took a while for Nigel to increase his sales numbers again, but he made progress. He still got to do the technical work that he loved. But, in order to keep doing it, he realized that he had to maintain relationships with the people who purchased from him.

Nigel's lesson is that sometimes you have to humble yourself. It's OK. Everyone has to wash windows from time to time. There are parts of all jobs for both employees and the self-employed alike that aren't much fun. Outsource them if possible. If not, do them yourself. Commit to getting unfavorable tasks done. If you persist in avoiding them you may have to look for another job.

Put a smile on your face.

How do you turn doing unfavorable tasks into a positive experience? For repetitive tasks, such as filing, put a smile on your face. Physiologically, it will put your body into a happier state. Play some uplifting music. Group similar tasks together and knock them out in one period of time each day or each week. Address the tasks before they accumulate—before you *really* don't want to do them.

For example, Alicia, the owner of an interior design business, intended to invoice her clients at least once a month. After all, that's where her revenue came from. But months would pass and she'd realize she wasn't getting her invoices done. So, instead of deferring her invoicing to the end of the month when it became unmanageable (she had to try to recreate what she had done for the client), she decided to try an "invoice on the spot" approach.

She'd tally her time daily and jot down notes in her Day Timer. At her last design session with the customer, she'd hand-write the invoice and make a copy for herself. Done. She'd eliminated the accumulation, burden, delay and inevitable errors of invoicing clients long after the work was done.

Hidden Trap 3: You Can't Make Me

"I could do it, but you can't make me."

"I resent it when my boss tells me what to do. I think, how dare he," said Philippe, a client of mine.

"How old is that conversation, Philippe?" I asked. "Is that the adult talking, or the child in you?"

"You know, I never thought of it that way. It must be like the eight-year-old in me," he responded.

When you take a job with a company, you are signing a contact stating that you will perform specific duties in exchange for a wage. When you are an employee, unless you are the CEO, you are a subordinate. This means you must follow direction in order to keep your job. Your boss is in charge.

This may sound obvious. But the You Can't Make Me Trap catches you because it implies that you should defy others and they cannot make you do anything. It's true, they can't *make* you do anything. But, if you choose to defy your boss, consequences will result that can jeopardize your job.

Like many other traps, the You Can't Make Me Trap stems from fear. It covers for you when you fear doing a job. Have you ever been given a job or project that extends beyond your competency and experience? You may resort to the You Can't Make Me Trap so that you don't have to confront your fear of doing the work. For example, Anna, a receptionist, received notice from the sales manager that she would now have to take sales orders directly. Previously these orders went to a sales representative.

She refused to take orders. "That's not the job I signed up to do. I'm not in sales and I won't take sales orders." Anna feared talking with people about closing deals. She didn't want to do it and clearly stated that no one could make her do it. What she did not say explicitly was that she was afraid to do sales—she didn't have the skills. She didn't want to fail.

Obviously, the sales manager wanted to expand Anna's role to include order taking. The manager, Sonia, wouldn't take "no" for an answer. Sonia offered to provide brief training to build up Anna's skills. Anna had a decision to make— do I do this new part of my job or continue to refuse to do it and face the consequences? You'll hear about what she decided below.

As Anna's story reveals, sometimes it's easier to refuse to do something than to admit that you don't have the skills to do it.

> **TIP:** Recognize when "I won't do it" is really a cover up for "I can't do it" or "I don't know how to do it."

Solutions for You Can't Make Me

Make adult decisions.

Be mature about it. Check to see who's running the show. When Philippe, for example, realized the eight year old in him was calling the shots, he had to make an adjustment by making *adult* decisions. Put your current self—the adult—in charge of your business and your career, not the eight-year-old in you. Know that when your boss makes a request of you, it's not personal—it's just a request that he or she thinks is necessary to get the job done.

Get out of your own way.

What's the greatest obstacle to your success? You. This is not to say that you're "bad." It is to say, however, that you are responsible. Along with being an adult and making adult decisions, you must learn to get out of your own way. Notice when "looking good" or "being right" become more important to you than success. This awareness will help you reduce your ego and make a sound choice.

For example, Deborah took a seminar to help build her on-line fitness business. In the seminar, the leaders instructed her on how to give a workshop to promote her fitness business. Deborah noticed herself falling into the You Can't Make Me Trap. "My mode of operation in life has been: Don't tell me what to do. You can't make me. I just started to notice it. I don't do it intentionally, but there it is again and again. I need to get over that!" Deborah said.

She became increasingly aware of the You Can't Make Me Trap when it came to developing her workshop. "I thought to myself, 'I'm a teacher. I know how to teach.' I could hear the voice in my head saying, 'You can't make me do it your way.' Then I watched myself procrastinate. I was putting off the workshop prep because I didn't want someone else making me do it."

When Deborah realized she had fallen into this trap, she stopped and reassessed her behavior.

"Finally, I just did the prep anyway." Deborah recognized that the knowledge from the seminar leaders would benefit her. Even though she had taught fitness classes before, she had never led a workshop. The seminar leaders shared their expertise based on their own training and experience.

Getting out of her own way paid off for Deborah. She stopped procrastinating and developed an excellent workshop that she delivered. As a result, she sold $2,000 in on-line fitness products and received the names of 12 people to follow up with who expressed interest in her programs. By climbing out of the You Can't Make Me Trap, Deborah produced results she'd never attained before. You can too, by building awareness and taking action to make sure that you get out of your own way.

Give yourself choices.

Choice moves you away from feeling forced and into feeling empowered. You have to do X. But, in most cases, you can choose *how* to do it. As long as you get the job done!

Ask yourself these questions:

- ✓ What choices do you have at work?

- ✓ What personal flair can you put into your projects?

- ✓ What can you do to make your projects your own?

By making the work your own, you can make the most of the opportunities your job presents. This will help you to learn, grow and develop new skills.

The ultimate choice for you to make is to either accept being an employee or become your own boss. If you cannot stand taking direction from others, you have the option of starting your own business or being an independent contractor, where you can produce work without a lot of guidance or direction. The independent contractor route, however, requires that you to be an expert in your field and not require supervision.

If you decide to work for a company, remind yourself of your agreement to be an employee and honor it.

Know the consequences.

Remember that solutions to the Adrenaline Junky Trap entailed tapping into the pain or consequences for you and others of putting things off to the last minute? Similarly, you need to look at the consequences of your choices when the You Can't Make Me Trap has taken over.

Before you refuse to do something at work, ask yourself this question: *What will happen if I don't do it?*

When the ego grabs hold of you, it won't be thinking of consequences. It's only interested in winning and getting its way. But you may not like the direction in which the You Can't Make Me Trap is taking you.

For example, the receptionist, Anna, originally responded to the new responsibilities with, "I'm not in sales and I won't take sales orders." She clearly conveyed that she had no intention of doing any sales and that no one could make her. When the Sonia, the sales manager had a one-on-one meeting with her, however, Anna quickly changed her response. Why? She found out the answer to the question: *What will happen if I don't do it?*

The sales manager told her on no uncertain terms, "Anna, if you don't do this, we will hire someone else who will." Begrudgingly at first, Anna agreed to take sales orders because she couldn't afford to lose her job. With training and practice, however, taking sales orders over the phone became second nature to her. She no longer dreaded the work and enjoyed serving the customers.

Take the initiative yourself to find out what will happen if you don't do something. From there decide what your decision is. If you see no penalty for not doing the job and no reward for doing it either, perhaps you will opt to not do it. But be careful not to make assumptions. Before you act on the assumption, "Nothing will happen if I don't do this," ask questions to make sure first. Know the consequences so you can make an informed decision.

Hidden Trap 4: The Self-Indulger

"I could do it, but I'd rather be sipping a latte."

"Too much is not enough."

—Irene Cara

Do you spend too much time at the coffee bar while projects pile up? Do you surf the net instead of answering important client calls? Do you extend lunch breaks, indulging in your favorite foods and having long conversations with friends?

As you learned earlier, the Couch Potato Trap involves doing nothing to avoid work. The Self-Indulger Trap, on the other hand, means treating yourself without working for the treat. It's like eating desert before dinner. For example, one business owner, Charles, decided to buy himself a convertible BMW before earning the money to pay for it. The bank soon drove his way and repossessed the vehicle.

The down side of The Self-Indulger Trap? Pleasure is fleeting. Working and overcoming obstacles to achieve a goal gives you deeper, more lasting satisfaction.

Solutions for Self-Indulgers

Because the Self-Indulger Trap entices you to luxuriate in rewards before work, you will need to develop new habits. Start by putting work first when you're working.

Work, then reward.

"Hard work pays off tomorrow, procrastination pays off today."

—Piers Steel

Do the work first. Reward yourself later.

For example, a new entrepreneur found herself watching TV four hours a day. She put off doing her work. She began to feel lethargic and work became less and less appealing. She no longer had a boss, so she could do what she wanted when she wanted—to her own detriment.

Finally, she decided to restructure her day. She rewarded herself with one hour (only) of TV after six hours of work. This worked and prevented her from starting her day with TV, which would then end up filling her whole day.

Remember to schedule it! You already know the importance of scheduling your time and sticking to it.

Give yourself mini-rewards during the day. Use your mid-morning break to take a ten-minute walk as a rewarding way to refresh your mind. Or order a book on the Internet or at the local bookstore near your office.

The point is to stay on track rather than whittling away at your day by constantly stimulating your senses. Focus your work time on work, knowing that you can enjoy yourself later without remorse.

Save the bigger rewards for outside of work. For example, did you launch the new product that you originally delayed for six months? Go out for a drink with your spouse after work. Go out to dinner with a friend. Get a massage. It's the difference between having a scoop of Haagen-Dazs as a treat after a job well done, as opposed to sitting at your desk eating a tub of it all day long. One is productive. The other is destructive.

TIP: Who's the person who interrupts your time the most? You!

Build your self-discipline muscle.

Self-discipline is the antidote to self-indulgence. Learning to stay in control of your actions and to tough out challenges instead of taking short cuts will give you the self-discipline you need to beat the Self-Indulger Trap.

"Discipline myself? Why would I want to do that?" you might ask.

The answer: So that you can get what you *really* want in life, not just immediate gratification. When you indulge, indulge, indulge you are dependent on each indulgence to make you happy. But the quick fix of getting something right now wears off quickly. You look forward to your next "fix" to feel good. (Or to prevent feeling bad!)

Most of my clients who want to overcome procrastination say they want to be more disciplined. Those in the Self-Indulger Trap, however, want the discipline without the effort. If only a magic blue pill would zap indulgence and produce discipline. If only… The pleasure-seeking ways of this trap will tell you to avoid pain at all costs. And, with change, comes discomfort, which means pain! But there is a greater pleasure to be had out of building discipline. When you learn how to move beyond instant gratification you will experience deeper satisfaction and gratitude on a continual basis.

Where do you find self-discipline? Inside yourself! When something desirable entices you, take a moment to decide. It may seem like you automatically grab one cup of coffee after another, for example, but you actually have a split second to choose each time.

> **TIP:** The new definition of self-discipline: Stop doing what hurts you.

Find the inner strength to walk away from over-indulgences that distract you from productivity. This strength will help you withstand difficulties and build character. Those are the qualities that you want and need in life. It will give you the tools to reject immediate satisfaction for something more sustainable and meaningful.

It will ultimately build your confidence and make you feel that you've contributed more to your company. You will gain a sense of pride in your work.

Making the shift from indulgence to discipline requires awareness and consciousness. The bridge to consciousness is asking the question:

Is the action I'm taking now producing the results I want at work?

Don't deceive yourself. Be honest. If you respond with a "no" ask yourself:

What can I do to produce results?

Your answer will include steps for getting back on track. For example, if the first question made you realize that you've been sitting alone in the break room munching potato chips for forty minutes, you have built awareness. To produce the results you truly want, you decide to go back to your desk write the proposal that's due the next day.

Self-discipline can have a positive ripple effect in your personal life as well. To use an extreme, consider the following scenario.

Bob spends two to three months a year on business travel. When he first started this, he noticed something startling—several of his colleagues had had affairs with each other.

Rather then keep this to himself and let it remain a secret temptation, when he returned back home Bob sat down with his wife and told her what was happening with his colleagues.

"I never want this to happen to us," Bob told his wife. "I want to talk to you every day on business travel to remind me of my commitment to you." His wife readily agreed to this plan.

Bob realized early on that he would have to have self-discipline to remain committed to his marriage—even when business travel brought temptation and opportunity. By being open with his wife and holding himself accountable, his self-discipline and delayed gratification paid off. He still has a strong marriage after 32 years.

> **TIP:** Tell someone else about your instant gratification urges to hold yourself accountable.

What are the larger goals that you're aiming to achieve? Focus on the big picture, not just what's immediately in front of you. Write your big goals down and keep them in sight to remind yourself to engage in activities that support your long-term and short-term goals.

Successful people apply self-discipline to their lives and their work. The ability to delay gratification and focus on what really matters leads to big rewards in life. Learning to build your self-discipline muscle will reduce the Self-Indulger Trap. Self-discipline will bring greater, more sustainable happiness without the ups and downs of immediate gratification.

Here are 5 tried and true ways to develop self-discipline. "I have a long way to go," you may say. That's OK. Take the first step. Building self-discipline *in any area of your life* will positively affect other areas as well. Choose one of these examples and apply it to your life for 30 days. Then add another.

1.   **Go the distance.** Park your car farther away from your destination. At work, choose the spot farthest away, not the spot by the front door. This will help you overcome physical resistance. This will

build your self-discipline by having you choose the more challenging route, not just the quick-fix solution of getting from point A to point B as fast as possible. Making things a little harder on yourself in simple areas will develop your ability to do things even when there's something much easier or exciting before you, such as a quick walk rather than the "trek" across the parking lot.

2.   **Face it.** Your boss has sent you an urgent e-mail: "In my office. Now!" You look at it, shut your office door, and busy yourself with talking to your best friend on your cell phone. Stop yourself. Realize you are trying to avoid the inevitable. Take a deep breath. Exit your office. Meet with your boss. Face what you fear. Develop the self-discipline to face unpleasant interactions. Don't hide out. Obviously, your boss can—and will—find you, which can worsen the situation.

3.   **Get healthy.** You know you need to exercise and you want to eat healthier. Usually you grab a hamburger and fries and eat it at your desk for lunch. Today you have a 30-minute lunch break. You want nothing more than to get an ice mocha at the corner coffee shop and veg out at your desk. Instead, grab the carrot and the bagel you packed for yourself. Head out for a brisk walk.

4.   **De-caffeinate.** How many cups of coffee do you drink a day? Reduce your intake by one cup per day. For example, if you normally drink three cups, drink only two today. Or drink decaf instead of caffeinated coffee for one week.

5.   **Think before you speak.** Sometimes you may find yourself blurting things out without thinking. For example, Simon, a passionate manager, found himself blurting things out at executive meetings to his own detriment. This behavior prevented him from getting a promotion. Before speaking, stop yourself. Ask: What do I

want to say? If you just want to stir things up, consider whether you really want to do that or not. Discipline yourself to speak wisely.

Keep building your self-discipline muscle—it'll create a barrier against the Self-Indulger Trap that pulls you to do the opposite.

Make the most of your work.

The Self-Indulger Trap lures you to do what you want to do when you want to do it. So figure out how to make work "work for you." Find a way to enjoy it. Think of why you *want* to work. Bottom line—make the most of each work day no matter what you're doing.

For example, Theresa started temp work at age 18. She found the work boring at first, but quickly learned she could get something out of every assignment. When she worked for the accounting department of a law firm, she used the opportunity to perfect her key-typing skills so that she could enter numbers efficiently without looking. When she temped at a real estate company, she mastered formatting business letters. At a consulting firm, she learned how to craft professional forms.

Because of her dedication to make the most of each opportunity, Theresa later became a skilled entrepreneur and business manager. Today, she manages her own staff because of all the opportunities she took advantage of back when the work itself didn't seem like what she wanted to do.

Making the most of your job will improve your skills and develop you as a person. And it will provide what the Self-Indulger Trap wants—enjoyment—in a positive way.

> **TIP:** Save your indulgences for the weekend!

Action Still Beats Procrastination!

Once you've identified any Hidden Procrastination Trap(s) you fall into, apply one or more of the solutions for that trap consistently each day. Once again, take action. Take any action. You'll be well on your way to putting procrastination behind you forever.

What's Next?

The final chapter brings the work of *The Naked Desk* together and empowers you to do just what its title says: Deliver.

Read on to discover how to meet your promises without doubling your time investment and how to build your reputation as a "can do" person.

chapter [6]

Deliver

How to Meet Deadlines and Make Decisions

"You can't build a reputation on what you're going to do."
—Henry Ford

DO YOU TAKE ON WORK ENTHUSIASTICALLY? Does the word "yes" leap out of your mouth before you really think? Does taking on too much lead to delay stress, and not doing what you say you'll do?

You may have been told to over-promise *and* still deliver. Do more. Produce more. Make it happen faster.

Or you may over-promise on your own. You want to do it all in a short time frame. But then your ability to deliver falls short.

Stop. Reassess the "yes" habit. Discover an easier way. These steps can help.

Step 1: Make Small Promises

Under-promise. Then actually deliver on your promises. If you still can't deliver, then you are still making unrealistic promises (or else you need to review Chapters 3, 4 and 5 on procrastination).

Make your commitment even smaller. Then deliver on that. How? Really examine what you can and can't do before making a commitment.

> **TIP:** Use the 24-hour rule. Wait 24 hours to decide on all of the extra work projects. Get back to the requester after you've thought it through.

Know the power of doing what you say you're going to do. It's better to under-promise and successfully deliver on time. People will recognize you as someone with high integrity who can "get the job done."

Step 2: Set Realistic Deadlines

Pam set a goal to write and distribute six sales letters in one week. Her boss encouraged her, "If you can do it, go for it!"

Pam wrote quickly, cranking out two letters in four days. She imagined the sound of the phone ringing off the hook from interested clients responding to her great sales copy. She pictured the bonus check in her hand from increased sales.

Writing away, Pam stayed late. She worked through her lunch hours. On Friday, she churned out yet another letter to advertise the company's new marketing seminar.

While she did accomplish writing three fabulous sales letters, Pam only met half of her original target. Why? She set an unrealistic deadline. She wanted and willed herself to make it happen, but there were not enough hours to produce on-time, quality letters.

Pam needed two additional weeks to write the remaining three letters.

"No problem," her boss said. "Remember, you set the original deadline. Just get it done."

"That's right. I did set the original deadline," Pam thought. "I have to be more realistic in the future. The added pressure isn't worth it. And I need to be able to get enough sleep during heavy work loads." She began to approach her deadlines more sensibly—to set herself up for success not failure.

Some of you, like Pam, get excited about accomplishments and set improbable deadlines. "I usually have no idea of what it'll take to get something done, especially if I'm new to the technology. So I just grab a deadline and go. This leads to problems down the road."

Can you relate? You may *want* to get better at setting accurate and realistic deadlines, but you need to know how to do it. Don't just pick a quick date and run around in a frenzy trying to meet it. Instead, apply these easy steps to master the art of setting realistic deadlines that you can meet.

Assess the hours it will realistically take.

How much work does this assignment entail? Pam knew from experience that the first letter would take 14-20 hours. The remaining five letters would take about six hours each. This is, of course, in addition to her other job duties. So, before she commits in the future, Pam needs to consider the actual hours it will take to get the job done. You too can use your experience to more accurately estimate the time you will need to complete a project.

> **TIP:** Assess the hours and then double them.

Ask questions. Get the information you need. Do you have people to help or are you on your own? What is it going to take to finish the project? Define the scope of the work to make an informed time estimate.

Think about each step of what needs to be done and set a deadline from there. What tasks make up the project? Brainstorm them. Write them down so that you know all of the pieces of the undertaking. If you jump ahead with the deadline without considering the details, your deadline will be arbitrary.

Be sure to include time for rework and problems that arise. For example, you may have a task list that reads: Design ad for new product. Be sure to include additional tasks such as Review design, and Create final design. Then you will be able consider the time it will take to draft designs first, rework the designs, and then deliver the final product.

> **TIP:** Logically break down all of the steps in your mind before you step into action.

Remember everything that's already on your plate.

You already have work and work projects going. Do you have room to add anything else to your plate? The task itself may only take two hours, but the question is, Do you have two hours to spare? You may opt to make a case for not adding anything else to your plate.

If you want to take on the task, but have no extra time, you will have to consider what you can remove to make room for the new assignment.

> **TIP:** Ask your boss, "Which of my projects is my number-one priority?" If you get another project when you're overloaded, ask, "What should I remove or delay to fit this in?"

If you take on the extra work without removing anything from your already-full plate the task will either take longer to finish or another task will suffer.

> **TIP:** Take on fewer projects to ensure quality on each one of them.

There are only so many hours in a day! If you take on more than you can possibly handle, you may not even finish the project at all, or you will have to rely on someone else on your team if you want to produce quality results in an unreasonable time period.

> **TIP:** There are 24-hours in a day.

Allow time for setbacks and resolving problems.

In the example above, Pam could have met her objective to write six sales letters. How? By giving herself two more weeks to finish.

Don't be overly ambitious about what you can squeeze into a few weeks or months. Be realistic. Don't make it more stressful than it needs to be.

Create a time buffer. Allow for setbacks, reworking parts of the project and resolving problems. Give yourself extra time to get things done. This goes along with under-promising. Even when you think you can get something done in a month, for example, add an extra week. You'll be glad you did when you inevitably need that extra time.

> **TIP:** Don't "schedule backwards." This trendy approach leads to missed deadlines. When you start with the end date and work backwards, you will tend to cram things into the allotted time period. Instead, figure out when you'll start the project and estimate how much time is needed to get the job done from this point forward. Chances are, the deadline you come up with will take longer to reach than the original deadline.

Sometimes when you realistically assess a task's duration, your deadline extends days or months beyond what management expects. What other solutions are possible? Think about increasing the budget. Think about adding resources. If you need to keep an aggressive deadline, for example, bring on more people. Or outsource pieces of the project.

You may also decide to narrow the scope of what you set out to do. Work with the customer on that. If, for example, you are designing a website, you could ask the client to provide all the "web-ready" graphics, text and other content so you can focus solely on designing the website itself.

Let the customer decide. Customers don't always choose the least expensive option. They want what they want, and they want quality. Negotiating what the project includes and does not include will set you up for success. It will also prevent the tendency toward over-committing, which can trigger procrastination or failed projects.

Step 3: Make Your Decisions Quickly and Effectively

What decision are you waffling on or delaying? How do you feel when you put off decisions? Do you feel weighed down? A sense of dread? Fear of making the "wrong" decision?

Putting off making decisions is one of the number-one ways to delay a project. Build up your decision-making courage and skill.

Decision making takes guts. Since you can't take all of the risk out of your decisions, get informed and then take action. Weigh the pros and cons. Then choose. Practice. You'll get better at it over time.

> **TIP:** Decision making secret—make a convincing guess.

The answer is *not* to hem and haw over every detail. Procrastinating on decisions will bog you down.

How to Make Effective Decisions

Effective means that you focus on a top priority and do it in a timely way.

Ask yourself: *What is the outcome I'm trying to achieve?*

For example, your boss offers you a promotion from Manager to Director. You have one week to decide.

Ask yourself: *Do I want to do this?*

If you respond with "yes," consider what's behind your wanting the opportunity. In the case of a new job, what do you want to get out of it? More responsibility? Greater respect? A sense of accomplishment? A higher salary for you and your family?

Then ask yourself: *What is the benefit of doing this?*

It's the "what's in it for me?" factor. It's your life. You can accept the offer or turn it down. Sometimes people get swept up in what other people want for them. For example, your boss might really, really want you to take the promotion. (And, be assured, there's something in it for him or her too!)

What do you want to achieve in taking the promotion? What would you do with more responsibility? Perhaps you want to take the company in a new direction. You also want to gain new leadership skills. What do you want out of more money? Is it about buying more things or improving the quality of your life through services such as house cleaning or hiring a fitness trainer?

Think about the downside of the offer. If you want less stress on the job and more time with your family, those factors will affect your decision. If, on the other hand, you want a raise to enjoy more expensive vacations, that will also have an impact on your decision. What's most important to you? What are your values? Answer from there.

> **TIP:** Just because you receive an offer doesn't mean you have to take it.

The above TIP might be obvious to you. But how many times have you said "yes" to something just because someone asked? How many times have you accepted an offer because it pleased someone else? Have you ever left your boss's office with your stomach wrenching because you just said, "yes" to something you dread?

Keep in mind that most decisions don't equate to prison sentences.

Remember that you'll have opportunities to course correct. Say you take the job and discover one month later that you don't want to work 14-hour days.

Time to make a new decision. For example, is there room to renegotiate hours? Or is there a better fit for in another department?

Also consider that you might make a good decision. A decision that forwards you, your boss and your company. Talk about contribution!

Avoiding decisions, big or small, keeps you in the limbo of non-action. Welcome to purgatory. Whether you consult with others or make decisions on your own, learn to be decisive and keep your projects moving.

Weak in this area? As with any underdeveloped part of you, you can use resources to grow. Read books like *The Naked Desk*, listen to CDs, consult a professional. I recommend the book *Harvard Business Review on Decision Making*, by Peter Ferdinand Drucker, et al. It's a potent book that breaks down how to make decisions and how to avoid decision-making traps. To succeed at what you do, you must learn the art of decision making and recognize how it can move you powerfully toward your goals.

Step 4: Leave Room for Creativity

Have you ever defined the scope of a project so narrowly that you boxed yourself in? While narrowing scope may be needed to bring a project in on time, be careful about overly defining every detail.

Why? You may come up with a better approach along the way. For example, a Pacific Northwest law firm hired me to lead a team-building event for its team. The firm wanted to improve communication, bond as a team and have a memorable, fun day. Initially, we met several times to go over which activities they wanted and develop a detailed agenda.

Midway through, however, I discovered that the event committee didn't have a clear concept of which activities might be better than others—they just wanted results. It's similar to hiring a graphic designer. You work with and tell the designer what you want and she goes to work on it. The designer probably will not go into *how* she will get the job done. She may use any number of design programs to deliver the effect you want and will probably come up with creative ideas along the way.

For the law firm, I decided to scratch the detailed agenda altogether. I said, "Let's move forward with this. I'll work on the design and deliver the outcomes you want: improve communication, build a stronger team and have fun. I'd prefer to deliver the final program design you when I see you at the retreat."

They trusted me enough to go along with it. My decision prevented me from being locked into pre-defined activities. For example, I initially thought having the people use plastic tubing to build geometric shapes and structures would achieve the results. I later scratched that idea and opted to use a lower-key exercise that uncovered each team member's values. It ended up being the most effective activity of the day.

Because I left room for creativity and innovation up front, I was able to deliver a better product to the client. At the end of the day, the group unanimously rated the event as their best training ever. Even the person who was initially most resistant said, "I used to despise trainings. What was valuable about today is that I learned that training doesn't have to be a torturous experience. I would attend an event like this any time."

The company immediately asked me to lead its next event for both attorneys and staff members. Leaving room for creativity led to a definite win.

Add oranges to your apples.

> *"The idea is to add a twist or an additional component to what the client expected: not just more, like eleven apples instead of ten, but tossing an orange in with the eleventh apple. The orange is something to surprise them with, but*

you haven't given them any fewer apples. Perhaps the client will be fascinated by the orange, decide they need more oranges, and that can lead to your next piece of work."

—Thomas Leonard, *The Portable Coach*

In the team building example, I was able to deliver the "apples" the customer wanted—several activities over a one-day period. Within that design I was also able to throw in some innovative activities and still help them improve communication and a sense of team—both within a fun and creative context.

Be sure to leave room for creativity in your own projects so that you can make discoveries along the way and innovate.

Step 5: Communicate Progress and Setbacks

"Be impeccable with your word."

—Don Miquel Ruiz, *The Four Agreements*

When you make progress along the way or experience set-backs—keep your customers and team in the loop. Communicate—the good and the bad—often.

Say you work in a corporate environment. You start a new project. You're enthusiastic and excited. The executives picked *you* to run it! You work on it feverishly for the next seven days. Then you get caught up in your regular work. The day-to-day customer hassles. The administrative tasks that *someone* has to do.

One day, you glance at your calendar. The project is due in four days. Because the executives haven't heard from you, they assume the project will soon be done. Yikes! You're going to miss your deadline!

Communicate. Now.

You communicate with the executives. They frown at the delay and lack of earlier communication. But they give you a one-week extension. Phew! They approve adding three more project team members. The team works every night and weekend to pull off the new deadline. With a little communicating, getting back on track and hard work, the project succeeds.

Most of you can relate to the above scenario. So, what can you do in the future to improve the odds of meeting the original deadline?

> **TIP:** Ever race to meet a deadline only to discover when you turned it in it didn't really matter? Distinguish between soft deadlines and hard deadlines. Hard deadlines, such as releasing a new product to the market, are serious. Focus on these deadlines first.

Remove time wasters.

Help yourself reduce setbacks by removing time wasters. Do you read your e-mail before you do your priority projects? Do you let people traipse into your office unannounced?

Once you set realistic deadlines, remove time wasters from your schedule so you can get to work and stay focused on your priorities. Build on the skills from this chapter. Practice your ability to focus, prioritize and take action to get the job done.

Sample time wasters:

✓ Constantly checking e-mail.

✓ Checking e-mail before high priority projects.

✓ Phone tag.

- ✓ Self-distractions, such as jumping to a website to order prints from your digital photos.

- ✓ Self-interruptions, such as responding to a text message from a friend.

- ✓ Listening to voice mail.

- ✓ Distractions, such as a loud meeting going on next to your office.

- ✓ Interruptions, such as people walking into your office unannounced.

- ✓ Not saying "no."

- ✓ Saying "yes" to too much.

- ✓ Sorting through junk mail.

- ✓ Opening spam and forwarded e-mail.

- ✓ Taking every phone call as it comes in.

- ✓ Not turning your phone off for work that requires concentration.

TIP: Set a specific time of day for returning phone calls and tell your clients that's when they can expect to hear from you. Respond to messages only during this time period.

Without time wasters you'll create more quality time for priorities. Fill this new time in with actions that will drive you toward your top priorities—toward results! When problems arise, face them head on so that they don't lead to delays. Get support. Get help.

Address missed deadlines.

Even when you eliminate time wasters, sometimes you still cannot bring an assignment in on time. You've worked hard. You've pulled out all the stops, but you realize your deadline will lapse. What do you do? Communicate right away and often. If it looks like you won't meet a deadline, give others notice right away. Put your ego aside and keep people informed and up to date.

Tell them what you've done to try to keep the project on track. See if they have additional suggestions to turn it around. Missing deadlines affects other people, such as your boss and your customers. Let them know ASAP. Don't turn your cube into a fort where you hide out hoping you'll miraculously pull something off.

In addition to communicating about missed deadlines, develop your skills so you can make good decisions along the way. Making good decisions will keep your projects from stalling and extending past their due dates.

What's Next?

By following the steps of *The Naked Desk*, you're well on your way toward being your best. Keep going. Don't let your progress stop here. Integrate what you've discovered into your daily life—on the job and at home. Don't wait for things to pile up again—paper, projects or poor use of your time—before you take action. Build on the momentum you've already initiated.

Thanks for your focused attention, time and energy. I hope *The Naked Desk* has inspired you to engage in a more rewarding work experience filled with ease, vitality and fun. I wish you the best as you move forward on your own!

What's next? It's up to you. Just take the next step. Whatever that step is for you. I'd love to hear about your experiences along the way. Send me before and after photos to reveal your new naked desks, your schedule with free time in it, and you smiling after conquering procrastination. If you need the support of a coach to help realize your goals, send me an email at: info@actionsymphony.com.

"Whatever you can do or dream you can, begin it. Boldness has genius, power, and magic in it."

—Johann Wolfgang von Goethe

Acknowledgments

This book evolved from the inspiration of the wonderful clients I have worked with since the mid-1990s. Thanks for your dedication and willingness to experiment with the techniques from *The Naked Desk*. Your ability to move forward and access your potential makes me know that I'm living my life's purpose. Thank you for that tremendous opportunity.

Thank you to my mentor—Judy Cullins. Your wit, energy, enthusiasm, and speed made this a fun ride. Also, many thanks to my editors: John Rashby-Pollock and Suzanne Schrag. This book wouldn't be the same without you. I appreciate your multitude of insights and ideas.

Thank you to Collette Searls for our brainstorming session that led to the title.

Thank you to Jerry Dorris at AuthorSupport.com for the cover design and quick turn around.

With gratitude to all the players that helped shape this book, you are all a dream to work with!

Quick Order Form

Secure Online Ordering: www.thenakeddesk.com

Fax Orders: 208-988-3577. Send this form.

Postal Orders: Ignite Press, 925 Freedom Boulevard, Suite 16, Watsonville, CA, 95076.

Email: orders@thenakeddesk.com

Questions? Call parent company Action Symphony at 831-239-9981.

The Naked Desk: *Everything you need to strip away clutter, save time & get things done.*

$14.99 US/ $18.99 CAN   ISBN 978-0-9789730-0-1

Books _____ x $14.99 = _____ + shipping _____ Order Total = _____

Sales tax: Please add 8.0% for products shipped to California addresses.

Printable e-Book available at www.thenakeddesk.com

Name: _____

Address: _____

City: _____ State: _____ Zip: _____

Phone: _____ Email: _____

FREE e-Zine, *Ignite Your Life*, available at www.actionsymphony.com

Please send me more FREE information on:
□ Coaching   □ Speaking/Seminars   □ Free Articles   □ Other books

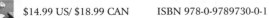

Shipping:

    USA: $4.00 for first book; add $2.00 for each additional item.

    International: $9.00 for first book; $5.00 for each additional item (estimate).

Card #: _____

Name on card: _____ Exp date: ____ / _____

Staying On Track
Other Services by Sue Brenner

How are you doing with applying the practices of *The Naked Desk*? You know yourself. Do you need someone to keep you on track? To challenge you? To hold you accountable so that you can get what you want most?

If you said, "yes" to any of these questions, work with a Performance Coach to guide and direct you. Sue Brenner's Company, Action Symphony, offers high-powered coaches to deliver the following services:

- **Free 30-minute Coaching Consultation**

- **Free e-Zine, *Ignite Your Life***

- **1-1 Coaching**

- **Small Group Coaching**

- **Coaching Programs (1-1 or Small Group):**

  - ✓ The Naked Desk in Action – *A 12-week action-packed coaching series to achieve everything you want from each of the chapters of the book.*

  - ✓ Career Track Pack – *Now What? 90 Days to a New Career Path*

  - ✓ Best Life Program

  - ✓ Relationship Toolkit

  - ✓ Leadership Path

To contact Sue Brenner and her team today, send an email to info@actionsymphony.com.

www.actionsymphony.com   www.thenakeddesk.com

Sue Brenner, PCC, PMP, Performance Coach and Author, wants you to get the most out of life and work. With fun, easy systems, Sue sparks people to ignite their potential. Since 1997, Sue has worked with Fortune 500 companies, top-notch small businesses and professionals to overcome obstacles. She serves as the CEO of the thriving coaching business Action Symphony and still loves to coach successful individuals and groups to reach the next level of success and beyond.

Her clients hire her across the globe, with an emphasis in Silicon Valley. They come from diverse industries—high tech, telecommunications, medical, bio tech, real estate, media, beauty and law. They keep sending new clients her way because of her dedication and passion for bringing out the best in people. The results? People accomplish higher productivity, deeper satisfaction and greater effectiveness on the job.

Sue writes free articles on business effectiveness and personal development to contribute to you—the reader. Find them at www.thenakeddesk.com.

Sue works and plays in the coastal community of Santa Cruz, California, with her husband and daughter.